Praise For *Trauma and  Informed Internal Family Systems*

This is a lovely, highly accessible and informative book for therapists who use the Internal Family Systems model of treatment. Those of us who have worked for many decades in the field of complex trauma and dissociation have become accustomed to the idea of needing psychotherapy approaches "plus" specialized understanding and knowledge about treating dissociation. Joanne Twombly has masterfully combined IFS and the basic tenets of treating clients with dissociative disorders, emphasizing that ego state "parts" and dissociative "parts" require somewhat different, if complementary, approaches. She offers pragmatic modifications of IFS to fit for more dissociative clients. IFS therapists will find a wealth of practical information illustrated by a variety of case examples. A must read!

Kathy Steele, MN, CS
Winner of 2017 Pierre Janet writing Award from the International Society for the Study of Trauma and Dissociation

This book is the missing link to integrating IFS with the treatment of complex trauma and dissociative disorders. It is needed on every IFS therapists' bookshelf!

IFS Certified Therapist and Client

This long-awaited book is for clinicians both as teacher and learner who are trained in Internal Family Systems (IFS), Voice Dialogue (VD), and other models of ego state psychotherapy and wish to enhance their competency to treat patients/clients with complex trauma and dissociative disorders. Joanne Twombly, by brilliantly demonstrating the use of basic IFS skills in concert with those skills from the world of complex trauma and dissociation, has provided new pathways for therapists to reduce their own stress while safely facilitating deep healing in clients/patients who mentally dissociate and develop high levels of anxiety and self-destructive behaviors even during treatment. Digesting these clearly written pages guides all therapists to integrate the evidence-based concepts and methods of subpersonality with those of EMDR, nonverbal and hypnotic communication, psychopharmacology, and psychodynamic countertransference. Twombly has provided a valuable resource for those who have the wish and courage to work with emotionally and physically traumatized children and adults.

John Livingstone, MD
Life Member of the American Academy of
Child and Adolescent Psychiatry
Assistant Clinical Professor of Psychiatry, McLean Hospital

Joanne Twombly's book is the missing piece of the puzzle in treating dissociative disorders. Her book is an invaluable guide for clinicians applying specific therapeutic modalities to work with patients who have complex trauma histories and/or dissociative disorders. Although attachment and parts work modalities such as IFS, Somatic Experiencing, Sensorimotor Psychotherapy, AEDP, have much to offer treatment of complex trauma and dissociative disorders, none is truly sufficient to navigate the complexities of a deeply fractured inner landscape. Joanne Twombly draws on decades of experience working with dissociative disorders to offer hard won wisdom and practical interventions to provide an essential tool for all trauma clinicians.

Kari Gleiser, Ph.D.
Senior Faculty Accelerated Experiential Dynamic
Psychotherapy (AEDP) Institute

TRAUMA AND DISSOCIATION INFORMED INTERNAL FAMILY SYSTEMS

TRAUMA AND DISSOCIATION INFORMED INTERNAL FAMILY SYSTEMS

How to Successfully Treat Complex PTSD and Dissociative Disorders

Joanne H. Twombly, MSW, LICSW

Trauma and Dissociation: Informed Internal Family Systems

Copyright © 2022 by Joanne H. Twombly, MSW, LICSW. All rights reserved.

No part of this publication may be reproduced, stored in a retrieval system or transmitted in any way by any means, electronic, mechanical, photocopy, recording or otherwise without the prior permission of the author except as provided by USA copyright law.

Adobe Caslon Text design by Carol Twombly.

This book is dedicated to every person in the world who has or has had a dissociative disorder. May you find the kind of therapist and healing you need and deserve.

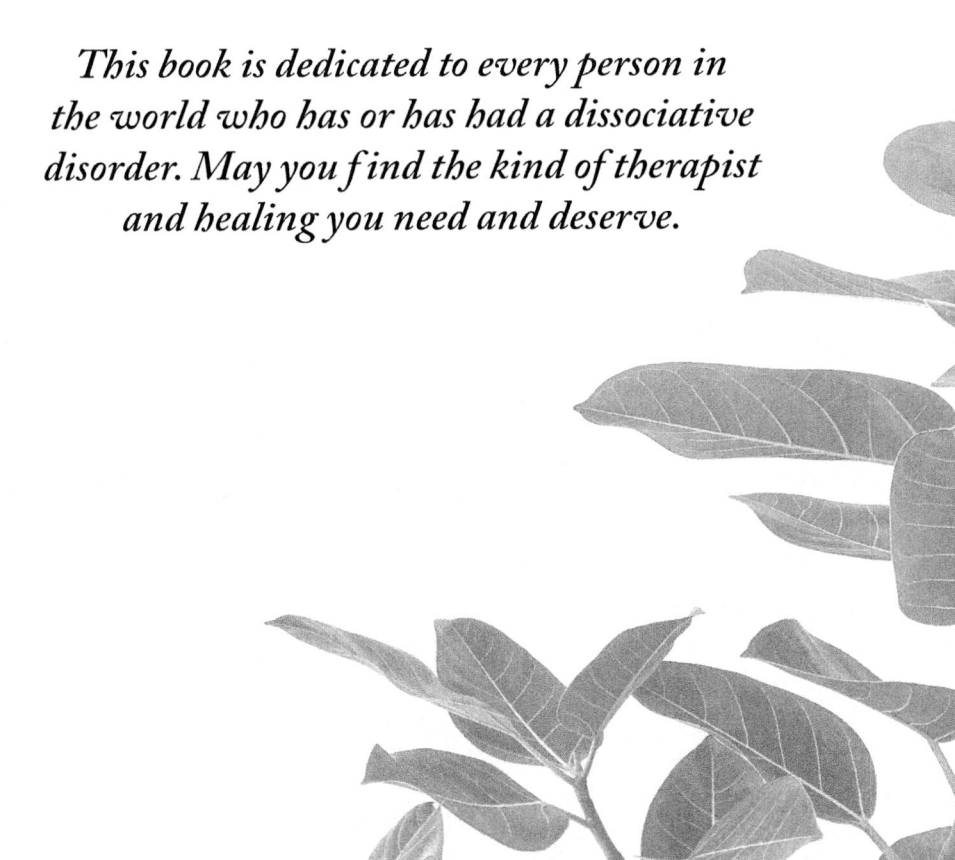

Trauma and Dissociation: Informed Internal Family Systems

Integrating IFS with the wealth of knowledge from the Complex PTSD and dissociative disorder world is where the power and healing are for clients with C-PTSD and Dissociative Disorders. If your client is getting worse, struggling during the week, and increasingly needs more support from you, the information in this book can help by integrating dimensions into the already excellent framework of standard IFS. You will learn to give your clients a chance to have more safety, control, and choices. They will heal more comprehensively and more efficiently by avoiding problems like increased anxiety, excess difficulty managing during the week, and increased risk of self-destructive behaviors. True, not every client will need the strategies and knowledge in this book, however, it's practical to be able to recognize when your clients do need them or simply can heal more efficiently with them. By reading this book you will gain the knowledge of how to treat these clients safely, respectfully, ethically, and successfully.

Want to learn more about how to manage trauma and dissociation? Two free handouts are available on Joanne's website: joannetwombly.net

Contents

Acknowledgments xiii
Introduction xv
Chapter 1. Gender, Race, and Culture 1
Chapter 2. Basic Summary of Standard IFS Including a Short History on Ego States 7
Chapter 3. Countertransference and the Fire Drill 20
Chapter 4. Hypnotic Language and Coping Skills 30
Chapter 5. Accessing for and Diagnosing Dissociative Disorders 71
Chapter 6. Dissociative Disorders 101 83
Chapter 7. Complex PTSD 101 93
Chapter 8. Memory 95
Chapter 9. Medication 98
Chapter 10. Introduction to Phase-Oriented Treatment 111
Chapter 11. Phase One: Establishing the Treatment, Developing Coping and Stabilization Skills 118
    Section 1. Daily Morning Homework *141*
    Section 2. Daily Life Teams *144*
    Section 3. Orienting Parts to the Present, also Known as Retrieval *150*

Chapter 12. Phase 2: IFS Witnessing and
    Unburdening: Paced, Protective and
    Productive Working Through of
    Traumatic Material 169
Chapter 13. Phase 3: Integrated Functioning,
    Adjusting to a Life Not Organized by Trauma ... 190
Chapter 14. Terminations Due to the Therapist's Needs 193
Chapter 15. Advanced Considerations 206
Chapter 16. Afterword 222
Appendix 227
Abbreviations 233
Glossary... 235
Bibliography 241
About the Author.. 253

Acknowledgments

I want to acknowledge:

My many mentors, including: Claire Frederick, MD, Richard Kluft, MD, Kathy Steele, MN, CS, Jim Chu, MD, Anna Salter, PhD, Bethany Brand, PhD., and Harvey Schwartz, PhD. Those of you I've worked with have made me the therapist I am. All have provided me pivotal workshops, have written pivotal books, and have done so with kindness and expertise.

Thank you, Richard Schwartz, PhD: For the IFS model as I never would have finished writing this book without unblending from the: "I can't do this/I'm not good enough" parts of me!

Special thanks go to Dan Brown, PhD, for help with the chapter on "Hypnotic Wording" and even more thanks for his impact on my life. I have been blessed to have gotten training and mentoring by him, as have all of us who work with trauma survivors and others. He is one of the people who took on the False Memory Syndrome Foundation and, always ethical and precise, he testified both for therapists who were being attacked and against therapists whose work was substandard. He was a role model during his life and dying process as he spent much of his last years in meditation practice and ensuring his attachment protocols and other works were available online. How do you say goodbye to one of your good introjects? I guess I don't have to because he will always be there in one way or another. RIP Dan.

Special thanks also go to Steve Frankel, PhD, JD for his help on the chapter "Premature Terminations," and to John Livingstone, MD for his help with the chapter on "Medication." In addition, thanks to Jackson Ravencroft, LICSW, Meg Striepe, PhD, and to Huge Kayma, MSW, PhD, MDIV, and Dip Phil for their help on the "Gender, Race and Culture" chapter.

Thanks also to my many writing consultants and colleagues: Lara Zielin, Writers Academy, who got me going; Ellaine Ursuy at Self-Publishing School who kept me going, Carol Grace who edited the first draft without whom I may never have managed to write this book, and gotten to my second editor, Corina Douglas at Burning Legacies Publishing, and last but definitely not least, to Paula Stanziani, a professional writer and editor who polished up the final draft. Also, to Carol Ginandes, PhD, Hillary Glick, PhD, Evelyn Gladu, LMHC, and the many other friends and colleagues who've read various versions and helped with encouragement and editing.

And finally, to my clients and the clients of other therapists whose struggles I've heard about through sessions, consultations and trainings. Treatment modalities don't work by themselves. It is the therapist and the client's work together that shapes and forms how they work. Thus, much of my learning has occurred in the many hours my clients and I have struggled together to understand and work through the horrors of their childhoods of abuse, neglect, and attachment issues along their path to healing. To them, I am grateful and full of admiration. Had I gone through the kinds of childhoods they lived through, I don't know that I would have survived as well as my clients and still had the capacity for love and the strength to strive for healing.

And of course, to my endlessly patient husband, Dave, without whom there would be no book and certainly less color in the world.

Introduction

How I Came to Write This Book

In the late 1980s when I was assigned my first client with Dissociative Identity Disorder (then called Multiple Personality Disorder), I'd read *"Sybil"* (Schreiber 1973), a book about a woman with MPD, but aside from that, knew nothing about working with clients with dissociative disorders. I was, however, in good company as the psychiatrist, the client's previous therapists, and the agency's clinical director knew nothing either. So, I began reading and attending workshops. Along the way, I learned hypnosis (dissociation is a trance state), sensory motor psychotherapy (abused and neglected children have to suppress and/or dissociate their feelings often resulting in them becoming adults with many somatic symptoms), Eye Movement and Desensitization Reprocessing (anything to speed up the processing of incredible pain), Cognitive Behavioral Therapy (correction of cognitive distortions is key) and then reluctantly, (reluctantly because I really thought I knew all I needed to learn about working with and healing parts of the mind) got multiple trainings in Internal Family Systems. Lo and behold, I found IFS was a brilliant addition to the mix of skills I already had.

These treatment models have formed the basis of how I treat clients with complex trauma histories. These clients, by virtue of the complexities of their childhoods and their individual styles of coping with those complexities, require a specialized knowledge base to treat them safely and successfully.

Who Should Read This Book

This book is written primarily for IFS therapists who treat C-PTSD and dissociative disorders. Actually, all IFS therapists will benefit from reading this book as will therapists trained in Voice Dialog, and other ego state models. Think of the Maslow's comment (1966), *"I suppose it is tempting, if the only tool you have is a hammer, to treat everything as if it were a nail."* IFS is wonderful hammer. Having other tools and ways of working will make your IFS work richer and give you more options when you need them. People with C-PTSD and dissociative disorders in IFS therapy or in other treatments may also find this book useful to read. One recommendation is to bring the book to therapy and ask your IFS therapist to read and work on it with you.

On Integrating IFS with the Trauma and Dissociation Knowledge Base

IFS is remarkable. The idea of cutting to the chase, doing trauma work, and bypassing resource work, without coping skills appealed to me immensely. It also works exceptionally well for many. But, as I initially used IFS with my complex trauma clients and provided consultation to IFS therapists and their clients, I found that people with C-PTSD and dissociative disorders needed coping skills to help them maintain functioning while going through the painful work of healing. Integrating IFS with the wealth of knowledge from the C-PTSD and dissociation world increases its power and the potential for healing. If your client is getting worse and worse, if your client is struggling during the week, if your client needs increasingly more support from you, the information in this book will help you by integrating dimensions that are missing in standard IFS training and practice.

In this book, you will learn to give your clients an ability to have more safety, control, and choices. They will heal more comprehensively and more efficiently by avoiding inadequate treatment that leaves layers of issues not attended to, and results in increased anxiety, excess difficulty managing during the week, and the increased risk of self-destructive behaviors. Although, not every client will need the strategies and knowledge in this book, it is practical to be able recognize when your client does need them or where adding strategies will make a client's healing more efficient. This book will assist you in gaining the knowledge you need to treat these clients safely, respectfully, ethically and successfully.

What IFS Therapists Will Get from Reading This Book:

- The ability to integrate the powerful treatment modality of IFS with the wealth of knowledge from the dissociative disorder/Complex-PTSD field.
- Strategies to strengthen and support managers' ability to manage.
- Coping and affect management skills for all parts that will help clients get through the healing process more efficiently while protecting their daily functioning.
- The ability to identify when and where your client is on the dissociative spectrum.

- The ability to use basic hypnotic language to enhance treatment, to recognize and use clients' innate trance abilities, and to enhance the use and impact of IFS.
- The ability to help facilitate your clients' parts growing and learning to work together.
- An understanding of the value and use in treatment of nonverbal communication, countertransference, projective identification, and reenactments.
- And finally this book will clear up some misunderstandings between the IFS world and the complex trauma/dissociative disorder world

Preparation for Reading this Book for IFS Therapists:

One of the gifts of IFS, is the format it provides for getting into Self in preparation for working with clients. Additionally, it will prepare you to be open and able to fully take in information, especially information that is new, and different from what you have been accustomed to hearing.

Check inside yourself and see if there are any parts who have concerns about reading this book and/or who are not open to learning new information and expanding belief systems. If there is a part, or more than one part with concerns, follow this simple process:

- Ask the part or parts to relax and unblend.
- Work with one part at a time, check for Self energy.
- Witness each parts' concerns.
- Find out what they need from you in Self to be able to let you read this book from a place of Curiosity, Centeredness, Calm, and Compassion.

I still think of this as the "Fire drill" process taught in IFS trainings to sort through countertransference reactions to a client. It was later reinforced in my *Intimacy from the Inside Out*/parts work with couples training with Toni Herbine-Blank, MS, RN, CS-P, where the same process was used to teach spouses to be able to listen receptively and talk to each other from Self.

Case Material

Much of the case material in this book has been offered freely by clients, most of whom have spent years in therapy with therapists who didn't recognize or know how to treat dissociative disorders or C- PTSD. Their hope is that therapists will learn to be able to recognize dissociative symptoms and disorders and provide adequate treatment so other people don't go have to go through what they have had to. Other examples are composites of actual sessions which retain the essence of the interactions, while protecting confidentiality.

Any mistakes and omissions are obviously all mine. Suggestions for further reading and learning will be made throughout this book and in the appendix.

CHAPTER 1
Gender, Race, and Culture

I am a white cis gender woman in her sixties. I grew up in an upper middle-class suburb, lily white enough that at age eleven, when I was assisting in a ballet class and had to correct an African American girl's posture, I felt uneasy and wondered if her skin would feel the same. In the past years, as I've taken workshops on gender and race inclusion and listened to people talk about their experiences, my eyes have been opened to macroaggressions, microaggressions and embedded racism that I didn't know existed within me. I've also learned about the fluidity of gender and range of possibility in normal relationships.

It is my hope that people of all races and genders will be able to read this book and benefit from it. I offer this chapter as an explanation for what I would have liked to have done and couldn't—make this an inclusive book, sensitive to gender, race and cultural concerns—and to provide basic guidelines and information. In that effort, I have consulted with Jackson Ravencroft, a transgender, non-binary social worker specializing in gender issues and trauma; Meg Stripe, a specialist in trauma, gender and sexual health; and Hugo Kamya, an expert in racial justice, social action and advocacy. Again, I take full responsibility for any mistakes I have inadvertently made and welcome feedback.

We as people and therapists need to constantly challenge ourselves to be in Self, curious and open to all ways that gender, race, and culture can be presented and experienced. We need to create space for issues that have been unspoken and at times, not even consciously thought about. We need to be able to speak about topics that feel different and uncomfortable, and take responsibility for our limitations, transferences and countertransferences. We need to maintain the ability to look inside our blind spots, to grow and change.

Gender Issues and Dissociated Parts

People with complex trauma and dissociative disorders can have parts who are male, female, gay, lesbian, asexual, robots, inanimate objects, animals, spirits, etc. Many are not sure who they are, and the question of "*Who am I?*" is ideally resolved in the therapeutic process.

One specific area of concern is that there are reported cases of people who have had a dominant part go through a gender transition, only to find out later that this was not a decision made by the whole person. Most of these people were given approval by therapists who did not know about dissociative disorders and gave them the standard body of psychological testing as part of the evaluation process. Unfortunately, standard psychological testing does not ask questions about or evaluate dissociation. I recommend that therapists who are evaluating people for gender reassessment add diagnostics for dissociative disorders and become competent in the standards of care for transgender and gender nonconforming people. Standards of care and the ethics of practice can be found online via the World Professional Association for Transgender Health.

How do you know if a dissociative disordered client should get gender reassignment? It takes time and openness for systemwide exploration, and one must allow for inevitable uncertainty and confusion before consensus is reached. One critically important question to ask is: how much of the wish to change genders is based on trauma and how much is based on a healthy expression of the person's identity, agreed upon by most or all parts? There is also growing concern regarding teenagers who feel that they are in the wrong body and who rush to get it corrected. Teenage years are when people feel all sorts of different feelings and emotions coinciding with neurological changes and developments.

There is no definitive yes or no here, just a caution to take time, negotiate with all parts and remain curious and open. It is best not to rush major decisions when a person has an extensive untreated abuse, neglect, and attachment disordered childhood, and has never had the experience of living a life not based on traumatic events and feelings.

Example: A cis gendered female was sexually abused as a child. A male part of her was dominant and "knew" he was not abused because he was male. The dominant male part got gender reassignment cleared by their therapist. In further therapy, DID was diagnosed, and as the system of parts was worked with, it became clear to the client that they belonged in a female body.

Example: A cis gendered male client with DID reported a history of feeling like a girl and secretly dressing in girls' clothing throughout his childhood. After systemwide discussions, they decided, with their therapist's approval, to start gender reassignment, which was very important to their healing.

Race

When I work with people of different races, I follow these guidelines:

1. Get into Self and be curious about what you don't know. Also, be curious about places in yourself where you may be blind to what you don't know.

2. Be open to acknowledging your knowledge base and your level of experience.
3. Ask about legacy burdens and their impact on the client's life and or traumas they have experienced due to racism.
4. Be aware of micro and macro aggressions and/or find out about them.
5. Bring up issues and questions about race, as clients may not be aware that you are interested or consider it important.
6. Be aware that some clients may not want to discuss issues of race or culture and may not need to.
7. Do your own research when necessary to avoid the risk of overburdening clients.
8. Realize that we in the USA have grown up largely in an atmosphere that is white centered. In her book *Me and White Supremacy: Combat Racism, Change the World, and Become a Good Ancestor* (2020), Layla Saad explains: "White centering is the centering of white people, white values, white norms and white feelings over everything and everyone else."
9. Realize that awareness and openness to change is key.

Culture/Language

Sometimes it is important to have clients in Self speak to exiles and child parts in their native tongue. As one client said, "It's the language of my heart." Even if the client's command of their first language isn't fluent, or that language was "exiled" by emigration factors, it may still be important to try. Many clients have found that their connection with and witnessing of parts is improved by speaking to them in their native language.

A final point about culture and language: There is often an idiosyncratic culture in the families of our traumatized and dissociative disordered clients. This is encouraged by adults as a way of isolating their victims, as in the messages: "No one will ever love you but us." "Everyone outside this family is dangerous." "Anyone who 'likes' you will abuse you." Language can be used idiosyncratically, for instance, "You're safe with me." (said by the perpetrator to the child). Another client was beaten for saying "The sky is blue." This is one example of abuse that left her with a mistrust of her perceptions and reality. Because children and trauma survivors tend to think concretely, the use of language in this book is intentionally concrete and clear. It is how I speak to clients as I want as much understanding as possible to reach as many parts as possible.

Summary

This has been a very quick overview of Gender, Race, and Culture both in the usual broad sense as well as within the idiosyncratic culture of dysfunctional families. I added this section as I do not have the breadth of knowledge to write this book while addressing these issues in the way they deserve to be. I find it interesting to work with people from different countries, races, and cultures, and those with different gender orientations. I wish people could find therapists who fit their needs, who know how to treat them, and who have knowledge of their specific gender and culture. Alas, that is rarely the case, especially for those who need a therapist with special skills or who live in an area without many options. On the other hand, sometimes the differences between myself and a client can mask deeper issues. For example, one woman announced that she would only meet with me if I was lesbian. I said, "I'm not, but let's give it a try working together anyway." She did, and we uncovered an important issue and resolved it. She had been abused by and was afraid of heterosexual women. Thus, if you and your client are a "perfect match" it might be important to ask about what would come up if he/she/they had had to work with a person of another ethnicity, or gender orientation. Sometimes bigger issues can be hidden in ways that seem perfectly normal and reasonable.

CHAPTER 2

Basic Summary of Standard IFS Including a Short History on Ego States

Introduction

This chapter consists of a short history on ego states to put working with parts into context, followed by a summary of standard IFS for people unfamiliar with IFS or who want a quick review.

A Short History of Working with Ego States and Parts of the Mind

The theory and practice of working with parts of the mind has a long legacy. A very incomplete list begins with the psychologist and physician Pierre Janet who pioneered work on phase-oriented treatment of trauma and dissociation during his career from 1898-1936 and is ranked one of the founding fathers of psychology. He was eventually followed by Paul Federn , MD who developed and wrote about the concept of ego states in his book, *Ego Psychology and the Psychosis* (1952); then by psychiatrist Eric Berne's development of Transactional Analysis and concept of the inner child, written about in the book, *Transactional Analysis in Psychotherapy* (1961). His work was followed by John Watkins,

PhD and Helen Watkins, psychotherapist's book *Ego States: Theory and Therapy* (1997) summarizing their work on ego state therapy. Like Richard Schwartz, PhD. during his development of IFS, the Watkins were heavily influenced by *"...techniques of group and family therapy and incorporated them to resolve conflicts between various 'ego states' that constitute a 'family of self' within a single individual (*Watkins H. 1993)." Many other theorists and clinicians have added to the wealth of knowledge in working with and healing parts of the mind in general and parts of the mind within clients on the dissociative spectrum.

One thing the dissociative disorder world has not accomplished and is a huge contribution of IFS, is to make working with parts accessible to many therapists who were never trained in any kind of ego state therapy. Through IFS, the knowledge that we all have parts has become more normalized and even popularized in a way that many therapists have learned and are learning about the power of working with parts of the mind.

Basic Summary of Standard Internal Family Systems

Internal Family Systems is an ego state model of therapy developed by Richard Schwartz and written about in his book initially published in 1995 and later updated in 2020. The fundamental principles are:

- We all have parts of the mind (the analytical part of me, the anxious part of me, the child part of me, etc.),
- Everyone has a core Self with solid leadership qualities and
- People are born with inherent healing wisdom.

> **Leadership Qualities of Self**
>
> - Calm
> - Curiosity
> - Compassion
> - Confidence
> - Courage
> - Clarity
> - Connectedness
> - Creativity

The theory behind IFS is that all parts of the mind, regardless of their external presentation, are dedicated to survival (this is consistent with other models of ego state therapy and parts work). Dysfunction occurs when parts become burdened with traumatic material (including unhealthy attachment patterns, and beliefs), and then become blended with Self (see below).

When parts become blended with Self, Self's energy and healing capacity is blocked. The IFS therapeutic process focuses on teaching parts to unblend from Self, thus freeing up Self to use its leadership qualities in the service of healing. Once all parts are healed, the person achieves balance and harmony within the internal system and can lead a Self-led life.

IFS's Concept of Self

The language of IFS is particularly useful in working with dissociative disordered clients, as is the IFS concept of Self when used as advised later in this book. Schwartz writes, "… the key to mental balance and harmony is to access our seat of consciousness, which we call the *Self*."(Schwartz 2020) Again the concept of Self has a long lineage of spiritual and religious traditions, for example Buddhism's "Buddha Nature", and different therapy models e.g., Hal and Sidra Stone's Voice Dialog developed in the early 1970s, and written about in the book, *Embracing Each Other* (Stone and Stone 1989). Schwartz's IFS has evolved this concept into a particularly useful treatment model and way of being.

IFS's Three Categories of Parts

IFS identifies three basic categories of parts including: exiles, managers, and firefighters.

- **Exile**s hold traumatic material or burdens. They are often child parts that experienced trauma and are isolated from the rest of the system in an effort to protect the client from the impact of their burdens (such as fear, pain, terror, shame, traumatic beliefs and material, etc.).
- **Manager**s are parts that run daily life and do their best to keep the system stable by protecting exiles from becoming triggered. Manager parts have many different strategies or patterns of behavior that function to keep life safe and stable. These parts may be codependent parts, controlling parts, workaholic, endlessly critical, people pleasing, etc.
- **Firefighter**s are parts that react in extreme ways when exiles become triggered, and managers get overwhelmed. Their role is to block exiles' traumatic burdens from destabilizing the client as quickly as possible. They may distract or block exiles' traumatic burdens by using drugs, drinking alcohol, self-mutilating, binge-eating, or any other way that distances or numbs.

Example 1: John had a history of child abuse. He sought treatment because he was drinking excessively, fell and broke his nose. He was an engineer who worked hard but was passed over for promotions. He was married to Mary who spent too much money on material things for herself and their two children. John could not say "No" to Mary or their children's requests. His parts included:

- Exiles who held burdens of terror, and the belief that if he ever said "No" everyone would hate, abuse, and abandon him.
- Manager parts who worked hard to manage the exile's fears by never saying "No". This resulted in John working long hours so his bosses would be pleased with him, and meeting whatever demands his children and wife made on him.
- Firefighter parts who showed up when his manager parts became overwhelmed and exhausted. They would drink heavily to block fear and overwhelm.

John's life had become a cycle of overworking, and endlessly meeting his boss', wife's and children's needs. This resulted in him becoming overwhelmed and exhausted, and then drinking to numb distress.

Example 2: Jamie was date raped in high school. Her mother had an anxiety disorder, and her father was an alcoholic. She began therapy after years of dieting and regaining weight. Her parts included:

- Exiles who held burdens of pain from feeling unloved by both parents, and traumatic symptoms related to the date rape.

- Managers who protected the system from the exiles' feelings by suppressing needs, being compliant, overly helpful, and endlessly friendly.
- And a firefighter part who binge ate when managers became overwhelmed, such as on a day when Jamie saw the rapist in the community. She became very triggered, and burdens of traumatic feelings poured out. As soon as Jamie got home, the firefighter part came out and binge ate. The binge eating blocked the traumatic feelings enough so that eventually the managers could take over again.

These two clients benefited from IFS as the overall goal is to achieve balance and harmony within one's internal system by freeing parts from their burdens, resulting in Self becoming an effective leader of the person's internal system of parts. When Self Leadership is achieved, parts remain unblended and provide input to Self, while respecting Self's leadership and decision-making.

The Seven Steps of IFS Therapy

Steps of IFS

1. Access Self
2. Witnessing
3. Retrieval
4. Unburdening
5. Replacing burdens with positive qualities
6. Integration and reconfiguring
7. Checking for Questions and concerns

IFS treatment consists of the following seven steps:

Step 1: Accessing Self

Accessing Self, or a critical mass of Self, is achieved by unblending parts from Self. It is important to let the part(s) know that the goal of unblending is so the client (and therapist) can get to know the part, and that there is no agenda to get rid of the part. When parts have concerns about unblending from Self, their concerns need to be addressed.

Originally, in IFS training parts were often asked to "step back" from Self. This wording is not recommended for people who have experienced abandonment, trauma, and neglect. Preferably, tell the client to ask the part to "relax and give you some space, so you (or we) can get to know the part."

To check for the presence of Self, ask the client: "What do you feel towards this part?" (i.e., the part that has just been unblended). If Self is present or present enough, the answer will be some version of the qualities of Self leadership, such as, curiosity, compassion, etc. If the answer is anything different from the qualities of Self leadership, it means Self is still blended with one or more parts. For instance, a client might say, "*I feel nothing.*" (This may be an indication that Self is blended with a part blocking feelings.) or "*That part is awful, I want to get rid of it.*" (This is an indication that Self is blended with a critical part).

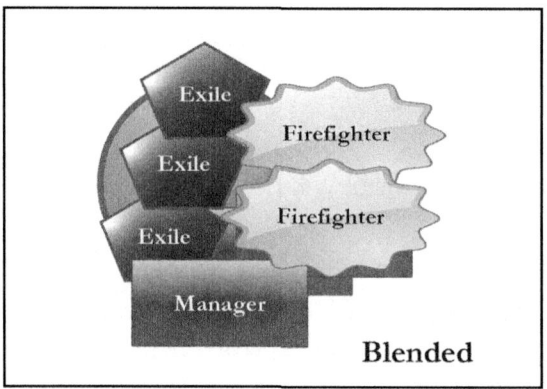

Blended

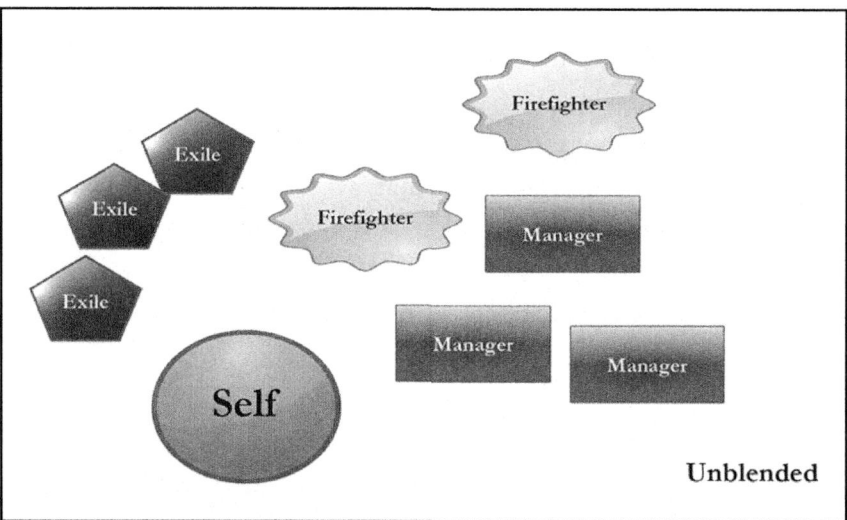

Unblended

Throughout IFS sessions it is important to check for the presence of Self. Sometimes clients will become reblended with parts and it's easy to check on this by simply asking, *"What are you feeling towards this part* (i.e., the part being focused on) *now?"*

Some clients have the felt experience that when parts unblend they actually separate physically. Other clients have a more somatic or in-body experience of parts. Either way, when there is a critical mass of Self present (i.e., when enough Self is present to begin learning to know and witness a part), the client will report feeling some of the attributes of Self towards the part.

Example: With one client you might be able to say: *"Focus on the panicked feeling in your body. Ask the part who is holding that panicked feeling to relax and give you some space, just like the part is sitting next to you."*

Example: With another client you might say: *"Focus on the panicked feeling in or around your body. What do you feel toward the part who holds that feeling?"*

Step 2: Witnessing

Once Self is accessed and the part who will go first has been identified, other parts are asked if they have any concerns with the work that is about to be done. Once the concerns (if any) are dealt with, witnessing takes place. Witnessing is begun by asking the client (in Self) to ask the part, what the part wants the client to know about them. The goal is for the part to feel and trust that Self knows and fully understands whatever the part needs Self to know. This includes information about burdens the part holds, feelings they suffer with, feelings they have towards themselves, beliefs, trauma, etc.

Example 1 continued: John's initial complaint was around his increased drinking. The manager part who drank agreed to unblend, and John showed enough Self energy by noting he felt curiosity towards the part. John was then guided to ask the part what the part wanted John to know about him. The part wanted John to know that he was helping John by managing overwhelming feelings and anxiety. He also stated that John would be a mess without him. John continued asking what the part wanted him to know and eventually found out the part didn't trust John to handle all his anxiety without drinking. An exile holding the anxiety was discovered. It was decided that this exile needed to be worked on before work could continue with the manager part who drank.

When the firefighter who binge-drank was going to be witnessed, his concern was that he would be forced to give up drinking. Through Self, he was assured that the goal was for him to have more choices and control about whether he wanted to drink or not. Later, when he had been witnessed, and was moving into the unburdening phase, his concern was that he would not continue to have a function. Through Self, he was assured that he would always have a function and could either decide what he wanted to do or together we could come up with a job for him.

At the end of the session, another part had concerns that John would be helpless without drinking. This part needed to be shown that John was an adult and then could be retrieved (see below) from the past and brought into the present.

Step 3: Retrieval

At times, before any witnessing or work is possible, the part must be retrieved, that is, brought from the past into the present. As long as parts believe they are living in the past, they tend to react as if the conditions in the past still exist in the present. When this is identified, Self finds out what the part needs to come into the present and attends to that.

Sometimes retrieval can be done after the unburdening phase, and/or it might automatically happen as burdens are released.

Example 1 continued: As John worked with the exile holding anxiety, he found out that this part believed that if he said "No" to anything, he would be abandoned and die. More questioning resulted in the realization that the exile believed he was living in John's childhood. Once the exile was retrieved, he could start to take in the current reality that John was an adult and there would not be any dire consequences to saying "No." Some of the part's burden of anxiety lessened with that and witnessing was continued.

Example 2 continued: Jamie had a part who had been taught that she would be killed if she ever spoke to anyone about the abuse she was suffering. This part needed to be retrieved before witnessing could be initiated. (See Chapter 14)

Step 4: Unburdening

Once the part feels fully witnessed, that is, when it feels fully understood and known by Self, the part is asked if it is willing to unburden whatever traumatic material it has been carrying.

I conceptualize clients' burdens as tangled webs of energy, that become neutralized when they are released. This conceptualization has helped clients who have worried that releasing their toxic burdens would "pollute" the universe. The client in Self is guided to ask the part how it wants to release the burdens. For example, "Do you want to let the burdens go into air, wind, light, water, fire, the earth, or in any other place or way?" One client of mine visualizes burdens flowing down a river, while another visualizes me helping her push them off a cliff. Another thinks this language is too "fluffy" and prefers to use some EMDR (Eye Movement Desensitization and Reprocessing) tapping to unburden his parts.

Example 1 continued: Once John's exile was witnessed, he felt okay to let his burdens of anxiety, old beliefs, and sadness go into a shaft of light.

Step 5: Replacing Burdens with Positive Qualities

As parts are freed up from burdens, they are asked what they are noticing, and are then invited to bring in whatever positive qualities they want and need. This is possible because the space formerly taken up by the burden(s) is now free. Qualities often noticed or taken in include energy, peacefulness, hope, trust, playfulness, and possibility.

Example 1 continued: John's exile noticed he felt lighter, and stronger. He realized he would not be punished for saying "No" and that he could ask John for help whenever he wanted. John also found that he had the energy to be curious about his children's and wife's needs and requests. He could consider and discuss them and decide if they fit within the family budget. He found he was able to say "No" when appropriate both at home and work. His need to drink diminished.

Step 6: Integration and reconfiguration of the system.

As parts are worked with and unburdened, the system of parts may become reconfigured. Parts who were always or often present, may become more relaxed and be less present. Parts who used to be managers or firefighters might move into a supportive or consultant status or develop a new position or job.

Example 1 continued: After John's parts were worked with, the firefighter who binge drank to protect John from anxiety and overwhelming feelings moved into a different role. He decided that he would watch for times when John should be assertive and prompt him to take better care of himself.

Step 7: Checking for Questions and Concerns

Throughout IFS sessions, the therapist periodically asks Self to check for parts that have concerns, comments, or questions. Each concern needs to be heard and addressed. This is also done at the end of the session.

It is helpful to ask parts who have been worked with, "*What do you need from me in between now and our next session.*" This step can decrease backlash and is also a way that the connection between the part and Self is reenforced.

Summary

This has been a very quick overview of the history of ego states and working with parts, and a very quick overview of standard IFS. For a more complete description of standard IFS read Schwartz and Sweezy's (2020), *Internal Family Systems Therapy, Second Edition*, and *Parts Work: An Illustrated Guide to Your Inner Life* (Holms 2011). More information about IFS and IFS training can be found in the appendix. Key to IFS is that when parts are freed from their burdens, balance is developed or regained within the internal system. Self then becomes the leader while parts are free to provide input, while respecting the overall leadership of Self.

CHAPTER 3

Countertransference and the Fire Drill

Introduction

This chapter will provide you with basic information on what countertransference is. It will outline how it can both interfere with treatment and be a helpful source of information about the client and/or yourself. The section on the fire drill will explain how to use this IFS process to both understand what the countertransference is about, and on how to use the fire drill to understand the messages within the countertransference and how to get into Self in relation to the client.

Countertransference

Countertransference feelings consist of:

- Nonverbal communications from the client
- Feelings you have in relation to a client that have something to do with the client
- Real feelings you have toward the client
- Feelings about working with the client that are triggering your own issues

Countertransference incorporates the analytic concepts of projective identification and reenactments, which are necessary to successfully work with traumatized clients.

Note: More information on projective identification and reenactments can be found in Chapter 15.

Because all of our feelings can get mixed in with the client's feelings and nonverbal communications, it is important to address any countertransference feelings that you are aware of between you and your client before using the fire drill.

During sessions it can also be useful to take a few moments to use the fire drill to sort out these feelings when the need arises.

Along with the fire drill, the following tips can help you when you are stuck in a countertransference/transference muddle with the client:

- Track your feelings and thoughts about the client.
- Be curious and ask the client, "What am I doing that is making things worse?"
- Say, "Let's look for patterns in our work and see if we can find some. If we do, I'm willing to look at my part and do my bit to unhook us…"
- Ask, "Does any of this feel familiar?"
- Own your part of it and apologize.
- Realize that this is a normal part of trauma dynamics and treatment. When you apologize, you model healthy and respectful communication with the client.

The following process describes how to do this using the fire drill exercise.

Introduction to the Fire Drill

The fire drill is a terrific exercise on sorting out countertransference feelings, getting clarity about a client, and for getting into what I think of as "your centered adult therapist Self." Generally, it is recommended to be in Self while working with clients. One caveat is that when working with clients with complex trauma histories, staying rigidly in Self is not a goal, as some of their communications will nonverbal and have to be experienced and felt to be received. This will be discussed further below.

When to Use the Fire Drill

1. Use before meeting with clients, especially those whom you have strong positive and negative feelings toward and/or those whom you have no feelings toward. Both positive and negative feelings can be the result of countertransference, so all feelings need to be checked out.

Note: Sometimes, when feelings and issues with a client are particularly difficult, it is best to do this exercise in a peer or consultation group, in your own therapy, or with a consultant. In any case, it is important to know (or to let whoever is going to lead you in the exercise know) that whatever comes up does not have to be said out loud. IFS can bring up sensitive information and confidentiality in our own communities of therapists is important.

2. Use while meeting with clients. Once you have practiced this exercise and have become familiar with it, it can be done in a short break during a session. Example: a therapist began feeling overpowered by a client. She said, *"Just give me a few seconds here, I need to sort something out."* She then identified that she was blended with a child part

who was triggered by the client being in a domineering state, reassured the child part, and continued the session with enough Self energy. This was helpful to the therapy, and role modeled for the client that when something is mixing you up or if you are blended with a part, take a break and get grounded or back in Self.
3. I also teach clients this exercise. It can be helpful in their daily life, e.g., to do before visiting one's family of origin, asking for raises, and before doing anything that brings up difficult feelings. Any occasion where a client might become automatically blended is a good time to do this exercise. Over time, clients will also learn how to use it during therapy sessions.
4. I use this the fire drill with all my individual consultees and in consultation groups when countertransference issues are present. Sometimes, it is what makes the consultation productive.

The Fire Drill Process

1. Visualize meeting with the client and the client doing and/or saying whatever brings up countertransference feelings.
2. Scan through your body and notice where you feel these feelings and somatic sensations (areas of tension, energy, feelings, etc.) in or around your body.

Trauma and Dissociation Informed Internal Family Systems

3. Tell the part or parts holding these feelings and sensations: *"I want to get to know you and hear what you have to say about this client. The easiest way to do this, is if you relax back, give me some space, sit next to me or unblend."*
   a. If there is more than one part, focus on the most present one or ask the parts: *"Who needs to go first?"* Once you have completed the process with the first one, check with the next one.
   b. If the part is unwilling to unblend, ask the part what the concerns are. Address the concerns.
   c. If other parts have concerns about parts unblending, deal with whatever their issues are.

      d. If the part is unable to unblend, focus on where you feel the part in your body, and continue below.
4. Check for the presence of Self energy. Ask yourself: "*What am I feeling towards this part.*" If you feel one or more of the Cs then you have Self energy. Remember, you do not need to have 100% Self energy, some is enough. Send the Self energy feelings (curiosity, compassion, etc.) towards the part.
      a. If you feel anything other than one of the Cs (e.g., anger, nothing, or negative) then you know you are blended with at least one other part.
      b. Let the part you started with know you'll be back, and shift to working with the part who is feeling anger/nothing/etc .
           i. Ask the part to give you some space and then check for Self energy.
           ii. Ask the part what the concern is about working with the first part.
           iii. Address the concern/s and negotiate with the part to let you work with the first part.
           iv. Or work with this part.

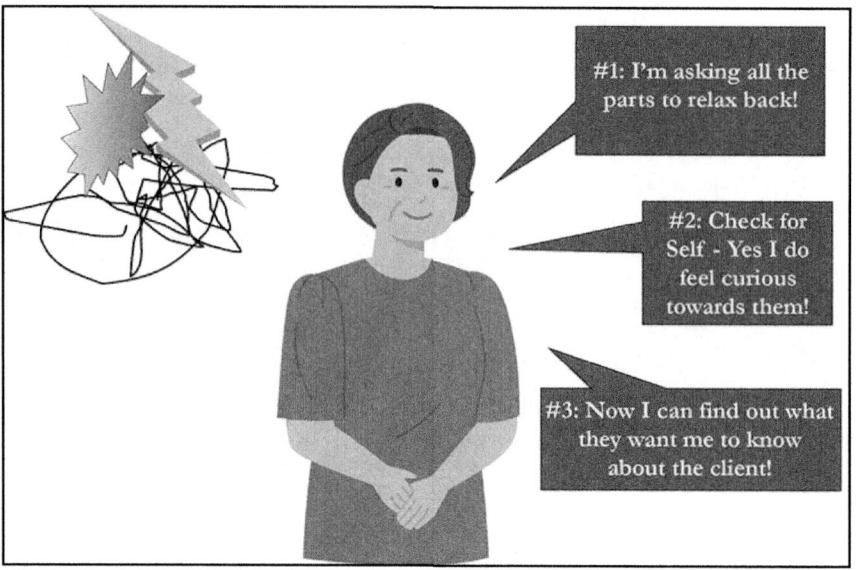

5. Again, focus on the part who is going to go first, and check that you have enough Self energy. Most IFS is done with a "critical mass" of Self energy which can be much less than 100 %. Send the part the feelings of Self energy (e.g., compassion, curiosity) and ask the part: *"What do you want me to know about this client and working with this client?"* Continue asking the part for information until the part feels fully understood and this focused witnessing is complete.
6. Then, ask the part: *"What do you need from me to let me handle the session from my centered, adult therapist Self?"*
7. Go through this process until each part who needs to be heard and understood has been fully heard and understood in relation to the specific client and anything else the part needs to have understood. Check yourself for Self energy as you begin working with each part and occasionally, as you work with parts.

8. Check back with any parts who had concerns including those who relaxed back and allowed you to work with others. See what comments, questions and concerns they have. See if any other parts have comments, questions and concerns.
9. Send all parts thanks and appreciation for the process they allowed you to go through with them.
10. Picture meeting with the client and check if any other difficult feelings come up and/or notice the difference.

Tips and Troubleshooting:

1. **A part of you may be carrying a large burden of material from your own childhood and as a result, may be getting**

triggered in session. It may help the part to be in a Safe Space during the session and/or to have a container to store that burden until it's the right time to work on it. (See chapter 4)

2. **A part may not trust you to handle the session.** The part may have a concern that can be dealt with or the part may simply not know how old you are. If the part thinks you are younger than you really are, ask the part to look into your eyes as you look into the part's eyes. Tell the part how old you are, something about your training and experience, and whatever else the part needs to know. Answer any questions. And say: *I've got strengths and resources I didn't have when I was your age."* This process helps parts begin to be retrieved or oriented to the present. (See chapter 11, Section 3.)

3. **Identify if you have been doing therapy from a parentified child part.** Many therapists grew up being parentified children, helpers, and/or having to manage many childhood issues on their own. These parts can easily become Self-like well-practiced therapist parts who do great work, but eventually become overwhelmed and burned out because they are child parts functioning in adult roles. Because these parts are so good at managing adult business, these parts can be hard to detect. Identifying these parts, unblending from them, and releasing them from the burden of this old job is important. Even if a parentified child is good at being a therapist, it is a child part, and will be working harder than a therapist in his/her centered adult Self. The part can still notice things about the client and be helpful but should not be in the therapist role.

4. **The fire drill can be very healing, although it is basically a quick fix.** Make a commitment to work on any childhood burdens or issues brought up in this experience on your own, with a therapist, or in a peer group. Keeping agreements made with your parts builds trust and will make it possible to continue to use this exercise productively.
5. **Check for Self energy before sessions, and during sessions.** If you notice you are not in Self, take a moment to use the fire drill to figure out why you slid out of Self, what it means about you or the client, and what needs to be done to get back into Self.

Summary

This chapter began with a quick overview of countertransference and then focused on how and when to use the fire drill exercise. It is particularly useful for therapists to use the fire drill when working with this population as these clients are living with dissociated and/or intense burdens of trauma and neglect, and grew up in families with distorted, twisted, and contradictory information. Consequently, communication may be obscured, nonverbal, acted out, or projected. To receive these communications, therapists must, at times, allow themselves consciously or unconsciously to slide out of Self, recognize that, decode the communication, and get back into Self. This may not happen instantly, but the fire drill will help this process be more efficient.

CHAPTER 4

Hypnotic Language and Coping Skills

"Words are the most powerful tool health care professionals possess. Like a double-edged sword, they can either maim or heal."

(Lown, 1996, "The Lost Art of Healing")

"Much of the "non-hypnotic" psychotherapy done today contains strong elements of spontaneous trance states and indirect hypnosis."

(Frederick and McNeal 1999
Inner Strengths: Contemporary Psychotherapy and Hypnosis for Ego-Strengthening")

Introduction

This chapter will teach you to use hypnotic language to maximize the impact of IFS (or any other therapy) in the healing process; to be knowledgeable about normal trances as well as trances resulting from child abuse; and to develop clients' existing trance behavior (i.e., symptoms) into coping skills.

This is particularly useful when working with people with PTSD and dissociative disorders where dissociative symptoms and trance behavior are often present, and with people with DID where it's unavoidable. As Kluft, (1994) stated, *"... with such highly hypnotizable patients, who spontaneously demonstrate dissociative and hypnotic phenomena and use defenses that incorporate these phenomena, it is impossible to treat Dissociative Identity Disorder (DID) without the treatment being suffused with hypnosis."* Learning to use what is not avoidable in the service of helping suffering people heal makes sense.

> **Note: PTSD is a biphasic disorder with alternating phases of intrusion and numbing.** *"This biphasic pattern is the result of dissociation: traumatic events are distanced and dissociated from usual conscious awareness in the numbing phase, only to return in the intrusive phase."* (Chu 1998)

Part 1 of this chapter provides information about hypnosis and trance states. Both normal occurring trances and those occurring in people with complex trauma and dissociative disorders will be discussed, along with the domain of hypnosis and hypnotically informed wording.

Part 2 of this chapter teaches how to use hypnotic language in the development of coping skills based on the client's ability to dissociate and hypnotic language. This is particularly useful in working with people with complex trauma where the goal is to maintain clients at their highest level of functioning (or higher if they have come in symptomatic). Destabilization can be often avoided by the judicious use of coping skills which facilitates the treatment process and enables the client to better manage their daily life and heal more efficiently. More about why coping skills are necessary with this population even in IFS treatment is discussed in this section and in Chapter 10.

Part 1
Hypnosis

Formal training in hypnosis (see appendix for information on hypnosis training) is extremely helpful and is recommended. However, as this population is often in trance anyway, hypnotic language can be used to teach clients to use the trances they are in, to help with stabilization, and eventually with witnessing and the unburdening process.

Hypnosis Definition: "*Hypnosis is a state of inner absorption, concentration and focused attention. It is like using a magnifying glass to focus the rays of the sun and make them more powerful. Similarly, when our minds are concentrated and focused, we are able to use our minds more powerfully. Because hypnosis allows people to use more of their potential, learning self-hypnosis is the ultimate act of self-control.*" (American Society of Clinical Hypnosis: www.asch.net)

The style of hypnotic language taught in this chapter is "permissive." With permissive hypnosis, the therapist facilitates the client's learning process, and uses imagery and language from the client to assist with developing imagery, suggestions, and coping skills. (Brown 1986). Hypnosis is the formal use of trance states.

The Trance State

Trances occur naturally. We all go in and out of them during our daily lives. Some examples of natural trance states include being "in the zone" (a trance familiar to anyone who watches or plays sports and video games), periods of intensely focused creativity or work, being absorbed reading a good book, daydreaming, and highway hypnosis (the experience of driving along a highway and suddenly noticing that you've driven past many more exits than you consciously realized). Relational trances happen when you are in an intense discussion or during an optimal therapy session when you and your client are on the same wavelength. In these trance states people are less distractable, for example, people may not hear you call them for dinner or may lose track of time.

Trauma related trances are also normal, as in the normal result of an abnormal childhood. In the section below on trance dynamics you will see that the following symptoms fit the criteria for trances as they are the result of inner absorption, focused attention, and dissociation.

- Flashbacks and anxiety attacks (e.g., peoples' attention become so focused that whatever evidence there is to the contrary is not noticed or may make no difference),
- Dissociative symptoms (e.g., having parts who are living in the past, mixing the present up with the past, losing time, not being connected to one's body, having the sense of other 'people' living in your body, etc.).

Children who are being abused are often in a trance as pain and terror focuses their concentration and/or they are required to dissociate to manage.

The use of trances can also be a learned behavior or acquired one through modeling parental trance behavior. When there has been intergenerational trauma, parents with untreated PTSD and dissociative disorders are often in and out of traumatic trance states during the day. Clients have described parents having flashbacks, traumatic nightmares, "swallowing their eyes" (presumably dissociating), and outright switching of parts. Sometimes abuse occurs in trance states. One client described his mother looking crazed, when she beat him until he was bloody. Once she got tired, she would switch back to "normal." Another client could easily identify when his mother was in an abusive part versus the "good mother" part.

IFS language and process lends itself to the use of hypnotic language as IFS's initial instructions to clients are like formal hypnotic trance inductions. E.g., "Focus inside and notice where you feel (whatever the client is feeling) ..." As you do IFS with your clients, you will often see them go into trance states. Because of this, the use of hypnotic language will enhance both standard IFS (and any other kind of therapy you do) as well as Trauma Informed IFS Therapy.

The Domain of Hypnosis

This list sketches out the domain or characteristics of hypnotic trances, including the domain of normally occurring trances from Daniel P. Brown and Erika Fromm's book (1986) *Hypnotherapy and Hypnoanalysis*. Think about your IFS sessions in general, and specifically about your complex trauma clients as you read through this section and notice what symptoms and behaviors are indicative of them being in trance states.

1. **Hypnosis and Attention**: Hypnosis is an altered state of consciousness. In an altered state, people will experience the world around them differently than in a normal waking state. They will be more focused, and less distractable.
2. **Suggestibility**: In trance people are more susceptible to positive and negative suggestions and their cognitive/thinking process is more concrete. This means that if something is stated negatively it will be heard negatively. For example, if a person is in trance and you say, "You will not die." The word "Die" may be focused on, leading

to panic. Wording suggestions using positive language is more helpful. "You are doing great." One client of mine was being transported by ambulance to the hospital after a bicycle accident. She heard the ambulance attendant say, "We're losing her." In the trance resulting from the pain, shock, and fear from her accident, she heard this literally and fixated on it. When she came into treatment for the resulting PTSD one of the most troublesome symptoms was "not feeling alive."

These techniques, often done naturally through the process of perpetration, are at other times used intentionally to trap their victim, increase their misery, and ensure that they will continue to be controlled long after their childhood has ended.

From *The Alchemy of Wolves and Sheep*

Harvey L. Schwartz (2013) "*A primary imperative of a perpetrator is to maintain the secrecy of the perpetration to insure the ongoing viability and sustainability of the abusive situations. From the single molester of a child to multi-member cults, they all use amnesia techniques (hypnotic suggestions, threats, shaming, drugs, classical conditioning, dissociation training) to erase the victims' memories of incidents, names, and faces.* (They also use) *many confusion, and amnesia inducing techniques... The power of all statements made during and immediately after abusive episodes while the victim is in an altered state will be enhanced by the absence of an operative critical consciousness and by the indelible connection with intolerable terror or dread...*"

3. **Altered Perception**: In deep states of trance, clients tend to be extremely involved with their own internal imagery and in whatever suggestions are intentionally or unintentionally given as in the inadvertent suggestion above given in the ambulance). Think of the belief systems of parts who think they are children and live as if the past were the present or parts of dissociated people who function as if they are deaf or paralyzed. Once a client asked me why I was raping her, as I was sitting on the other side of the office fully clothed and not touching her. She was perceiving the external world through absorption of her inner world. Another client worried that her father, dead for many years, would hear her if she told me about what he had done to her.
4. **Time Distortion and Timelessness**: Parts may think they live in the past and the past is still happening, that dead perpetrators can still abuse them, or that your vacation will last forever. This trance dynamic will be used later in this chapter in coping skill Deep Dreamless Sleep.
5. **Dissociation:** Dissociation simply means that some of one's experience is kept out of one's awareness. For instance, we all carry pools of information within us that we have pushed off to the side, such as how to tie shoes, or drive a car. These are complex actions that once fully learned and practiced, we do without thinking. The information is not lost, just compartmentalized, or dissociated. Dissociation is also used by people like emergency medical technicians (EMTs), police, emergency room physicians, nurses and surgeons. For example, to function at the sight of a car crash with bloody, severely injured children, an EMTs must cultivate a certain level of dissociation to remain functional. An additional example is when a person has recall of an event

but the affect, somatic sensations, behavioral components are dissociated or obscured. Dissociation can be thought of as a skill or an automatic defense that helps children survive difficult childhoods, but this "skill" can evolve into crippling symptoms. Dissociative symptoms include amnesia for the past or events, parts having knowledge other parts do not have, numbness, depersonalization, derealization, etc.

6. **Trance Logic or Tolerance for Incongruity:** This can lead to mixed up perceptions and what Kluft refers to as "Multiple Reality Disorder." One of my clients had a part who knew what year it was and that she lived down the street from my office in Massachusetts. However, as soon as she walked in my waiting room, she believed she was in another state, in fourth grade, living with her parents, and being abused every day.

7. **Perceived Involuntarism:** Dissociative clients experience this "watching" themselves do something they do not want to do and cannot stop doing, "hearing" messages like "you're bad" coming from what feels like nowhere, and parts who are experienced as external to the body, and/or are out of the client's control, etc.

8. **Change of Body Image:** Examples of this include looking at one's adult hand and seeing a child's hand, seeing nothing in a mirror, and an adult having the perception of being a child's height and not being able to reach something at easy reach for the adult person.

9. **State Dependent Learning:** Since much of the act of abusing a child results in the child being in a trance state, it is important to take into consideration state dependent learning. If we learn something in a particular state, generally it is more difficult to have total access to that information in a different state of being. Long

term alcoholics find that in sobriety, behaviors that were once automatic while drunk feel unfamiliar and have to be relearned. Similarly, reworking and healing lessons learned while being abused is facilitated when the treatment makes use of trance states.

Hypnotically Informed Wording

This section will provide knowledge on the impact of wording. This is important to keep in mind when doing IFS with clients who had to unconsciously practice their trance ability over and over to survive their childhoods.

1. **Watch for idiosyncratic negative responses to words.** Perpetrators sometimes use words and twist their meaning. For instance, a perpetrator who regularly says, "You're safe with me, we're going to have fun and play." That child may have an idiosyncratic response to the words "safe, fun and play." At some point these words will have to be normalized, but initially, it is best to substitute non-traumatizing words and to apologize if you use them accidently.
2. **Use wording from the client's representational systems.** People filter their information through three representational systems. Identifying your client's representational system and using words from that system will provide the client with the most connected experience. Identify which representational system your client uses by listening to them. Clues include:
    a. Visual: "I see", "I'm a big picture person."
    b. Auditory: "I hear you." "I hear your voice telling me…"
    c. Kinesthetic: "I feel your pain." I feel like this should be done differently."

3. **Link suggestions**: Linking suggestions are statements where the first part is something true and is then linked to what you clinically want to have happen. As these clients are often in trance states, this kind of statement will help develop coping skills e.g., "As you store traumatic material in the container, the container will get stronger and stronger." Linking suggestions are also used in the form of posthypnotic suggestions, for example: *As we struggle to figure things out, you will understand more and more... As the child part is in her safe space, she will be learning more and more about how things are different now... As you practice coping skills, you will find more and more ways they can help you manage your daily life...*

   Linking suggestions are also used (like everything) by perpetrators. Example: A client who had been done with treatment for some months came in for an extremely chaotic, confusing emergency session when a deeply dissociated part got suddenly triggered. This part held the following message from her long dead sadistic father, "When everything in your life is great, you have friends, a good job, and pets you love that's when I'll come and get you."

4. **Repetition**: The hypnotic law of Concentrated Attention states that repetition focuses. When attention is focused on an idea or a pattern it tends to result in it happening. *The more and more we work on this the more and more we'll figure it out. It will get easier and easier to find ways to practice.*

5. **Concrete thought processes**: In trance people are very concrete. In addition, most child parts have childlike vocabulary. It is best to communicate clearly and concretely and to use vocabulary that the whole system will understand.

6. **The "Yes set":** If you ask a series of questions where the answer is yes, it makes it more likely that the next question will also be answered "yes." Example: *Do you remember when we worked on that awful experience you went through in nursery school? You thought it was hopeless that you'd ever feel better about it! We worked on it step by step, and now it feels really different! We're going to work on this trauma now until it's healed and feels totally different, okay?*
7. **State things with a soft, secure confidence.** Express feelings but not intensely. If you praise someone or act too concerned or too understanding, some parts may think you are trying to deceive them. Pay attention to how you client reacts to your style of wording and adjust it if necessary.
8. **Use positive suggestion.** People who are brought up with lots of negative messages, criticism, and hopelessness will often answer "no" if you give them the opportunity. For example, saying "Try and see if you can find a safe space," "You may see...," will often result in the client saying, "I can't" or "Nothing is there." It is best to use positive suggestion, "What's a place or a space that feels safe..." or "What are you noticing..." Note: I do have one client for whom positive suggestion does not work at all. With him I say, "*What do you think about the possibility of seeing if that part might want to try Safe Space Imagery (SSI)?*" Nothing works for everyone and it is important to listen to our clients' feedback and have the flexibility to try different things until you find something that works.
9. **Posthypnotic type positive suggestions**: Give suggestions to increase the possibility of unconscious progress during the week, for example: *As time passes, parts will learn more and more about how things are different now...* (an orienting to the present comment), or *As you practice SSI, you will notice more and more times when you can use it...*

Part 2
Coping Skills

Why Learn About Coping Skills?
IFS Doesn't Believe in Coping Skills!

Survivors of complex trauma and the kind of trauma/neglect that results in people with complex dissociative disorders have burdens that are volcanic. Parts may not want to overwhelm Self or may think they can tolerate witnessing, but they may lack the knowledge to make this decision as the information might be partially or totally dissociated. Therapy done with people after they have been overwhelmed in standard IFS therapy by skilled IFS providers makes this clear. It is important to assess who can heal through standard IFS, and who needs Trauma Informed IFS. In the latter category, I put people whose treatment, life during treatment, and healing could be smoother and more efficient with coping skills, and people for whom standard IFS runs the risk of opening up too much traumatic material too fast, destabilizing them and creating backlash.

A goal is to keep clients in the window of tolerance.

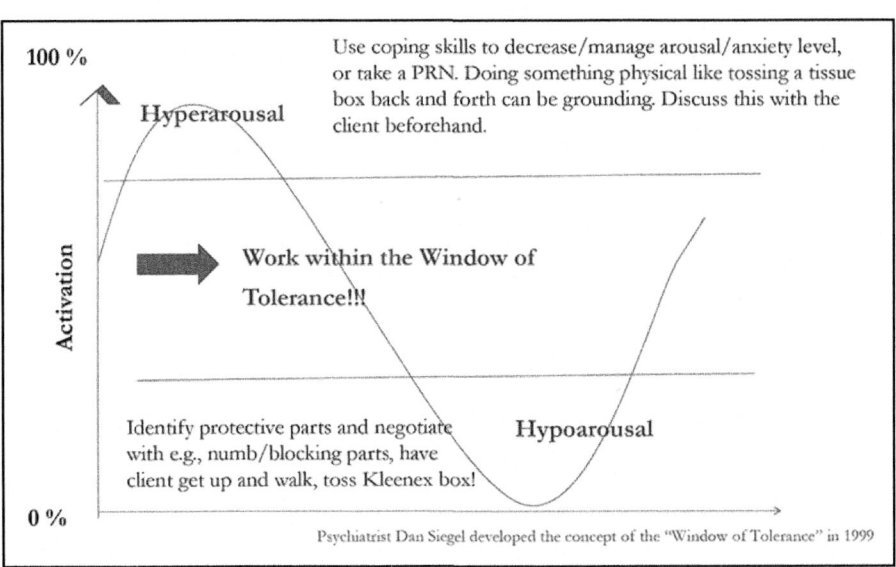

I often show clients this graph and we talk about what coping skills they can use when they become hyperarroused (experience flashbacks, heightened anxiety, racy thought patterns, frequent shifting of parts, etc.) or hypoarroused (numb, unresponsive, thoughts occur at a slow pace).

The coping skills taught in this section are widely used in the trauma and dissociation field to help people maintain or improve stability in their daily life and manage symptoms while going through the painful work of healing. They work differently than frontal lobe/left brain coping skills like distraction (find 10 green items in this room), and cognitive strategies (which take concentration and work), and coping skills like imagery, relaxation and meditating which can result in an increase in intrusive thoughts and feelings for people with unhealed trauma histories. Coping skills can and have been used productively within the framework of IFS to provide extra support for weary managers, overactive firefighters, and overwhelmed exiles who carry extreme burdens. They provide skills clients can use to manage backlash and triggers during their daily lives, overwhelm during sessions, and to increase their level of competence, control, and choices. Eventually, these coping skills are used to help with the witnessing and unburdening of traumatic material by titrating it, i.e., working on it chunk by chunk.

Hypnotic Language Recommendations

This section provides a list of ways to facilitate hypnotic language and/or the trance people are in already. Many can be used during therapy. Others are described in terms of the development of coping skills like Safe Space Imagery (SSI).

1. Keep track of words used by the client and use them. This is an integral part of teaching coping skills. It also

helps with development of the treatment relationship, as it means you are listening.
2. Involve as many senses as possible to make the experience richer.
3. Facilitate and support communication with the client (and parts) through-out exercises.
4. Use positive suggestion to anticipate and guide the client toward positive responses.
5. Reinforce success with ego-strengthening comments.
6. In trance people are concrete. Make suggestions general not specific. For example, "Whenever the time is right" versus giving a specific time.
7. Pause to give clients time to visualize or imagine and learn clients' rates of response. (I follow suggested language with "…" to indicate a place where it may be helpful to allow a pause for the client to take in your words or respond.
8. State things in a quietly confident and positive way. Avoid negatives and words like "try."
9. It's best to utilize imagery, wording, and feelings that come from the client, but if the client is blocked, it can be helpful to offer suggestions based on your knowledge of the client.
10. Like a posthypnotic suggestion, give suggestions to increase the possibility of unconscious progress during the week, e.g., *"As days pass you will find more and more ways to use Safe Space Imagery…" "As time passes you (or all of you) will learn more and more about how things are different now…"*
11. **Make sure you bring your client out of trance and ground them back to the office when the session ends.** For example, say, *"Take a few moments and bring yourself back here now. Look around my office make sure you're here…"* An ending the session routine can be helpful. With

one client we agreed to always talk about computers as this pulled forward an adult part.

Hypnotic language will be further taught through the process of learning the extremely useful coping skill Safe Space Imagery (SSI) (Kluft, 1989, Brown and Fromm, 1989, Morton and Frederick, 1997, Twombly, 2001). This coping skill and the others taught in this chapter teach clients to evolve their dissociative symptoms into coping skills, thus utilizing something that has been troubling for healing purposes.

> Erickson, M. 1980. Utilization Definition
> *"...The development of a therapeutic situation permitting the patient to use his own thinking, his own understandings, his own emotions in the way that best fits him in his scheme of life"*

The following coping skills will be detailed below:

- Safe Space Imagery, including variations
- Bubble Imagery
- Containers
- Establishing Safe Walls
- Affect Dial
- Deep Dreamless Sleep

Coping Skill: Safe Space Imagery (SSI) Kluft, 1988

SSI is a relatively easy exercise taught in the stabilization stage of trauma treatment, that provides hope for healing, and can be used as the cornerstone of the treatment process for clients with dissociative disorders. I introduce it early on by putting it into the context of the healing process.

> Note: Normalize whenever possible, as these clients tend to feel different and defective.
>
> Note: SSI and many imagery exercises should NOT be done while driving unless there is or are parts that are fulling oriented, present, and are doing the driving.

This process is specifically designed for clients with C-PTSD and DDs (Twombly, 2001) and is done through direct access. This is a trimmed down version of the version I learned in hypnosis training as it makes use of the trances these clients are already in. The language used is concrete and basic as trauma survivors think concretely, and child parts often do not have the range of adult vocabulary. It channels people into positive imagery because it is very easy for these clients to slide into negative imagery due to childhoods filled with critical messages. Choices are given to the client. This is an important part of healing for those whose childhoods were filled with needs that were ignored and "choices" that were often manipulated, e.g., a girl being given the "choice" of killing a bunny or being beaten, another client given the "choice" to be sexually abused or to let his baby sister be sexually abused. Suggestions of imagery are provided, if necessary, as some people's ability to fantasize or be creative is stymied by their need to shut down thinking to protect themselves from traumatic imagery.

When teaching SSI (and other coping skills), ask all parts who are willing, to watch and learn how to do it. Healing cannot all be done in sessions and this is one way to facilitate healing during the week. Examples of adapting SSI for different kinds of parts will be given later in this chapter.

Psychoeducation on the Benefits of SSI for Clients

I start out by giving clients psychoeducation on SSI. It is an exercise that will help the client learn to reach a state of relaxation and block out intrusive thoughts and feelings. From information I know about the client, I state evidence that suggests their future success. For example, I might say, *"We're sitting together in my office, there's nothing bad happening here right now, and you're feeling anxious. Right now, you are importing anxious feelings, which means you have the ability to take feelings from somewhere else and bring them here. We're just going to use your ability to import feelings in the opposite way, to import positive ones. It's just like a muscle that needs practice."* To a client who remembered nothing before the age of 11. I said, *"You have already been able to unconsciously block out everything before you were 11. Now we're going to work on you learning to block out things in a conscious way to help with your healing."* These kinds of comments begin to reframe some of the symptoms that brought them into treatment as abilities they will learn to use to help with the treatment process.

Other psychoeducation includes: *"In practice, daily use of Safe Space Imagery helps normalize the body's biological arousal level, which gets stuck in high gear during childhoods filled with anxiety and depression. This results in clients and their systems of parts being able to reach a deeper state of relaxation and with practice, to feel calmer overall. Managing daily life, and eventually the witnessing and unburdening process, is easier when one is calmer overall. In a good enough childhood, children develop a foundation of security and confidence, that if something goes wrong, things will get better. They also learn how to deal with strong feelings through having parents who can manage strong feelings. For those of us* (note: normalizing) *who didn't get that, doing SSI every day begins to build the foundation of security and confidence children get when they grow up with healthier parents."*

> Note: Some clients think learning coping skills isn't doing "real trauma work." I tell them: *"Working on developing coping skills is working on trauma because it is teaching you what you didn't get back then. It gives you control over symptoms and your life in a way you've never had. Trauma work is not just working on the really bad stuff, it is building in what's missing."*

Also normalizing is to tell clients, *"Research recommends that we all do some kind of safe space imagery, meditation, and/or progressive muscle relaxation every day as it strengthens our immune systems and makes us healthier."* (e.g., Segerstrom and Miller, 2004).

Safe Place Imagery will be a helpful coping skill to have once trauma processing is begun, both to provide respite from intense negative affect and to help center the client following the trauma processing part of the session.

Predict the possibility of intrusions as best as you can, without suggesting them. This normalizes intrusions as part of the learning process and decreases distress over perceived failure. One way of expressing this is, *"Sometimes people immediately get a safe space which feels safe. For others there will be intrusive images and that will give us a chance to work on you having practice dealing with them. Either way, we will figure it out."*

I recommend practicing wording in this exercise out loud before using it with clients. It can also be helpful to practice it with a colleague to get a sense of pacing and process.

Teaching SSI

All parts need safe spaces, including any part that identifies as or appears to be Self, as the likelihood is that this "Self" is more of a Self-like part, carrying burdens and blended. For these clients "Self" having a safe space helps consolidate Self energy and provides respite when this part, who tends to be the one running life, is tired. Some clients have one safe space for all parts, some have different safe spaces for parts or groups of parts who have different needs and preferences. In practice, I find that some parts need their own safe spaces or if there is only one safe space, it might have many different areas for different parts. For instance, one client started out with a safe space on a mountain top. This was eventually expanded to include a cave system with different rooms and nearby mountain peaks for other parts. Another client used a condo complex with different condos for different parts, or groups of parts, and a common area for gatherings/meetings. A bowling alley was added for child parts who needed some entertainment.

SSI Process: Wording and Comments

First tell your client: *You can keep your eyes open or closed, or experiment with what's best for you.*

Pick a place or a space not from your childhood	This instruction guards against concrete compliance. Some people immediately have flash backs if asked to close their eyes and if compliant, will not know that they have the choice to open their eyes.

Where nothing bad has ever happened.

For some, the safest time was right after abuse had occurred, and they knew it would not happen again that day or night. It is important not to replicate this, as this kind of "safe" space also tends to get contaminated rapidly.

Where you have felt safe or would like to be able to feel safe, or a place or space that's completely or partially made up.

The goal is a positive, calm, relaxed physical state not factual accuracy. The choice of safe space may not make sense to the therapist, but there is always a reason for it. For example, one client chose "nowhere" because no one could hurt her there. Another client's SS was in a coffin as their father wouldn't look for them if they were dead. A teenager chose in the middle of a soccer field.

Problem solving: If a client has trouble thinking of a place or a space, I offer them some suggestions: a beach, mountain top, an island, another planet, surrounded by music, or soft blankets. Use any information the client has told you in crafting your suggestions.

It's best if images come from the client, but sometimes it needs to be a joint process.

Look around your safe space with all your senses and notice everything about it that makes it safe to be there.

Note: This process front-loads for safety. Use of as many senses as possible to enhance the experience. It's important to remember some people are not good at visual imagery and may need to use other senses.

Perhaps you could describe what you're noticing... As you notice the (e.g., trees, sunlight, and that no one is there) keep looking around with all your senses and you'll notice more and more...... The client might have noticed for instance, that she is alone on a beach, she can feel the sun, and hear seagulls... The therapist can repeat this back to her by saying: So, you're on a beach, you can feel the sun and hear seagulls...

Note: 3 dot's indicate pauses to allow the client to visualize or focus. Everyone has a different rate of response.

Look around your Safe Place with all your senses and notice if there's anything you see (hear, smell, taste, touch) that doesn't feel quite right and if there is, just look around and as you look around, you'll either see (hear, smell, taste, touch) something that will help, or some thoughts will occur to you that will help

This step anticipates intrusions and begins the process of teaching the client to handle them.

Ask: *What are you noticing?... Focus on it and notice what changes...* or *Notice what thoughts come to mind...... Focus on them and notice what changes...*

In trance there's increased access to imagery and increased problem solving. Most of the time, even in a very light trance, this will result in the client being able to look around and something helpful showing up, or a helpful thought popping into the client's mind.

You're just learning this technique and already you have been able to get rid of some of that intrusion...

Note: This is an ego-strengthening comment.

Keep looking around and you'll notice something else that will help...what are you noticing... focus on the (light or bird) and notice what changes...

Carefully watch and listen for clients who can't get rid of intrusions. When this happens, I work on it with them by making suggestions to add or subtract something that makes it safer. If the first safe place can't be made safe, I will either ask if the client wants to continue, or suggest that the client is *"leaving this safe place and getting closer and closer to a new safe place that's even safer..."* This is teaching the client a problem-solving process to deal with intrusions as they work on Safe Place Imagery at home. For example, the process would go something like this:

1. *First look around and you will see something that helps.*
2. *If that doesn't work, then a thought will occur to you...*
3. *Or try adding something like a friendly guard dog, or a Forcefield or subtracting something that doesn't work.*
4. *Or move to a new safer Safe Space...*
5. *Or try drawing a picture of it and draw in improvements...*
6. *If nothing works, no problem, write a note about what was happening and we'll talk about it the next time we meet and figure it out.*

Once a client has reached a place where they can relax and feel totally calm, say:

As you're settled in (whatever the safe space is*) breathing in and out all the feelings of being* (use client's words for feelings) *and let all the feelings settle deep inside you, to every cell of your body.*	E.g., *"As you're settled on the island sitting in the sand breathing in the scent of the ocean feeling relaxed and peaceful, breath in all the feelings of being relaxed and peaceful, and feel those feelings settle deep inside you, spreading to every cell of your body."*

| | Research has shown that trauma has an impact on a cellular level (van der Kolk, 1994). This suggestion is made to suggest both the possibility of cellular repair and the message that the body is learning to relax deeper than it ever has been able to. |

Allow the client to focus on the feelings internally for 30 seconds (or less), as long as they look calm.

You've just started learning this and already you're learning to create an environment in which you can really relax… and as time passes you will find more and more ways to use SSI in your daily life…

As you start to wrap up the exercise give the client an ego-strengthening comment and posthypnotic type suggestion that fits the client's experience.

OK, now come back to the present. You might want to stretch your arms and legs out, move around a bit.

This step starts the process of realerting the client and having them return to the present fully out of the imagery.

Or, if the client still seems in some kind of a trance, you can say, *I'm going to count backwards from 5 to 1 and when I reach 1 you'll be back in the present fully aware and alert.* As you count, start softly, and raise the level of your voice so you end louder. *5...4...noticing the changes as you come back to the office at 3....2...notice you're (say what you're noticing, e.g., breathing differently, or moving around a bit) and 1 totally back in the present...* It is important to make sure the client is out of trance

And then we discuss how the process went for them, and I answer any questions they may have. The goals of SSI are to create a place or a space that the client can feel totally safe, comfortable, and relaxed in, and to be able to adjust it or create a new one as needed.

Clients are instructed to practice Safe Place Imagery everyday whether they feel stressed or not. Because traumatic material can be dissociated, some clients may feel quite "centered" during the week because everything distressing has been dissociated. The purpose of practicing is so the skill is available when it is needed. I often tell clients that no one would ever consider driving on a highway before spending time practicing in parking lots and on quiet streets. Practicing Safe Space Imagery when it's not needed increases the chance that it will be useful in crisis or during trauma processing.

Example: David, a client with complex PTSD, started out with a safe space on a beach. It was safe because it was familiar, sunny, warm and relaxed, and he was sitting on a beach chair reading. As he looked around with all his senses he realized the water was freezing cold and there were no lifeguards. He felt alert and watchful because someone could need his help... As he looked around with all his senses, he noticed a lifeguard. As he focused on the lifeguard, he noticed he felt peaceful and relaxed again, because everyone was being taken care of.

Note: Doing SSI with clients can indicate problem areas. This person was quite codependent.

Instructions for Parts

For clients with complex PTSD and DDS I start out by telling them the goal is that all parts of the mind have a safe space either a group one or an individual one, it doesn't matter.

It's often useful to ask one part to volunteer to try out SSI while all other parts watch and learn how it is done. The intention here is that hypervigilant parts who do not trust me, are given permission to watch me and see that I'm not doing anything bad to them. I am also encouraging a non-trauma based use of the need to be hypervigilant in that besides keeping an eye on me, they can use it to learn how to do SSI really well. Once I have a volunteer I may speak directly to the part: *"Ok great, I'm going to talk directly to Ahmed now and everyone else can watch and see how it's done. Ahmed now pick a place or a space...etc."* Or, I may have a part with some Self energy speak to the volunteering part to develop the SS. *"Sara, ask Ahmed to pick a place or a space..."* It depends on what works best for the client, and for the part we are working with.

Once we've finished, I ask all parts including the part who worked on it to talk about what it was like and to ask any questions they have.

A common therapist error is to assume that if you do SSI with one part of a dissociative client that all parts will automatically be included. This rarely happens. Parts need to be spoken to directly or they won't think it applies to them. One possible indication of an undiagnosed dissociative disorder is when a client has successfully learned SSI in session but cannot access it at home. One reason this can happen is that as the client does SSI at home, parts become anxious because the part doing SSI is relaxing, therefore putting all in presumed danger.

Variations

SSI for Young Child Parts and Baby Parts:

An older part with some Self energy can make a safe space on behalf of a young part. Ask: *As you focus on the baby part, what's a place or a space she can begin to feel safe in?* If the older part has no ideas to start with, I often suggest, *What about a room with a soft carpet, soft stuffed animals, with just the right kind of light and temperature?... What does this feel like for the baby part?* That might work, or it may help the client come up with other ideas. To continue say, *Look around the space and notice that all the things the baby needs to be safe and comfortable are there... What are you noticing?...* As always, support the client in doing as much of their own imagery as possible, but be ready to become an active participant if necessary. A good posthypnotic suggestion for these safe spaces is, *As the baby's needs develop, the baby will notice that everything she needs is there...* This suggestion indicates that the safe space will continue to develop. Also useful as an orienting to the present kind of suggestion is, *As the baby rests in the SS she will be learning more and more about how things are different now...* Homework for the client is to check on the baby part every once in a while during the week (whether the baby part stays in the safe space or not). Next session, I also make a point of checking in with the parts about how practicing SSI went during the week.

These child SSs can be a simple and elegant way of accomplishing many tasks at the same time with a minimum of effort. Elements I routinely suggest are:

1. A developmentally appropriate environment that gives the nonverbal message: *Your needs are important and will be paid attention to.*

2. Suggestions that healing is taking place can be added with healing light or music, or (one of my personal favorites) "Ativan air" so with every breath the baby becomes more and more relaxed and calm… If the client is familiar with Ativan, the concept of Ativan air can be helpful, and works because of trance logic and somatic memory. Note: Ativan is a sedative often used on a PRN or as needed basis.
3. Orientation information can be assisted by a safe space with a one-way window or a webcam through which the part can watch older parts manage their present life. No one had webcams when they were children, so as they see the webcam, they know things are different. Other orienting suggestions are a picture of the house they live in NOW, or a calendar with dates of therapy appointments listed.

The following examples describe different kinds of safe spaces.

Developmental Safe Space

One client had a part who was a rock. The safe space for this part was a bare cement room. This sounded harsh and punitive to me, however, the client said that the rock part didn't deserve anything nicer, and besides, the rock part felt safer in it. By the next week, the safe space had a thin carpet on the floor. As time passed and burdens were worked on, the rock sprouted little arms, legs, and a head, then became a little being, then a little boy, then a bigger little boy. During this process the safe space got progressively more comfortable. Eventually, it became linked to another safe space with other little boy parts who he could visit and play with when he was ready.

Process Safe Spaces

A process safe space is one where something needs to happen. For example, If a child part is weeping, terrified, or tantruming the safe space can be a soothing environment for the child to become calmer in. It's basically the same kind of environment that would help an actual tantruming child. Sound- and feeling-proofing can be added to the walls, so the SS can remain quiet and calm for the child, and the other parts are protected from the feelings of the child part.

Safe Space for a Spirit Part

A client had a part with no body and explained, *"If you don't have a body, you don't get hurt."* The SS for this part was a very strong bubble filled with light and positive feelings, with a hammock for the part in case it needed a resting place. As the part felt safer, it eventually developed a body.

Safe Space on Another Planet

This safe space was created for a part that the client hated. The client was coached to say to the part, *"I don't like you, and I want you to go away, but Joanne says that in order to heal, I have to get to know you. I'm not ready to do that yet, but I guess I'll have to."* (Note: In this example, the client recognized the presence of this part, and recognition is a bit of Self energy.)

The space for this hated part had a protective dome around it. An evil spirit flew in. The client looked around their safe space with all their senses and noticed an aerosol can. After focusing on the aerosol can, they said, *"Oh, it's giggle juice. I just sprayed it on an evil spirit, and the spirit was laughing so hard, it forgot about me and the little part and floated away."*

Protective SSI

Safe spaces can be used to protect the part (or parts) in it, or to protect others from the feelings of that part(s). Dani came in for a consultation on his IFS therapy. In the last twenty minutes, he mentioned he had to go to court the next day and was anxious about it, because as a child, he was beaten until he confessed whether he had done anything wrong or not. We identified the part who held the need to confess and checked for Self energy. Dani created a safe space for this part with (a) soundproofing, so the part didn't have to hear anything going on, and (b) feeling-proofing, so he didn't have to feel anxiety from other parts and they didn't need to feel his anxiety. I asked Dani to ask the part if he would be interested in staying in his safe space and not going to court. The part said, *"You mean I don't have to go to court?"* and happily stayed in the safe space until court was over. No other parts had any concerns. This speedy intervention made a big difference in the outcome of court, because the client was able to be more centered in Self and could represent himself fairly.

Secure Safe Space

At times, there are parts who are or might be dangerous. It is very important to take all threats of violence seriously to provide for both our own and the client's safety. With care, I have used the process in the following example with a few clients. Francis had a group of homicidal parts and a history of acting out violently. Three eleven-year-old parts with enough Self energy worked with me to make a secure safe space for these parts. The safe space was dropped over the group. It was very big and moved with the group, so the group never reached the edges of it and never knew they were in it. Positive suggestions included, "As the parts move, the walls get stronger and stronger, and the parts automatically get the message that things are different now. No one is allowed to hurt them, and they are not allowed to hurt anyone or themselves." Over a number of sessions, the eleven-year-olds witnessed manageable amounts of what the homicidal parts were burdened with, starting with "a tiny drop." As the witnessing and unburdening progressed the parts inside the secure safe space became calmer.

Safe Space in the Past

Although I recommend beginning with a safe space that is in the present, sometimes it is not possible. The following dialog took place with a client whose frantic child part insisted that the only safe space for her was a treehouse in the woods near the home where she grew up. In the treehouse, the child had always felt safe.

Once the child felt safe in the treehouse safe space, I suggested, *"Clara, focus on the safe space and the trees around the safe space and bring it into the present."*

Clara said, *"She causes too much trouble, I don't want her in the present."*

Therapist, *"Ok, so bring the treehouse out of the past and closer to the present. It doesn't need to be all the way in the present."*

Since this was okay with Clara, I continued with, *"Now look around the safe space with the child and notice there are things in it like a current calendar, with our appointment dates on it, and a webcam so she can watch you, get to know you, and learn about the present when she wants to."*

Clara: *"She doesn't know what a webcam is."*

Therapist: *"Ok, as you look around the treehouse, you'll notice something that helps her use the webcam... what are you noticing?"*

Clara: *"It changed into a red and blue plastic child's webcam with an on and off switch. She likes it!"*

Therapist: *Great, I'm glad! And as she's in her safe space in the treehouse, she'll learn more and more about how things are different now..."*

Hospital Safe Space

Some parts carry burdens of somatic pain and injuries from abuse. A hospital safe space can be used to create a healing environment. For example, several small parts held burdens of very painful somatic and emotional feelings. Their safe space was in a hospital in a foreign country far away from the parents who had abused them. They were attended to by African American Buddhist nurses as their family was Caucasian and rigidly Catholic, these nurses felt safe and nurturing. They were given "pain pills" and were surrounded by healing music. They stayed there until enough of the other parts had been witnessed and unburdened, and there was enough systemwide energy to begin helping them. By that time, they had rested enough and were feeling better in general.

Coping Skill: Bubble Imagery

Bubble imagery is a coping skill that is portable. For some clients or parts you can simply suggest: *Picture that you're surrounded by a bubble that's got all the feelings of your safe space in it… Now, notice it's getting bigger and smaller and smaller and bigger, and experiment with that until it's just the right size.* Or you can have a part in their safe space and say: *Notice there is a bubble floating closer and closer until it's around you. Notice it's getting bigger and smaller till it's just the right size for you, and that all the feelings of your SS are in it… Look around the inside of the bubble and you'll notice more and more about it that makes it safe… As you focus on the bubble it gets stronger and stronger… and notice that the bubble is made of special material that lets good vibes in, and keeps bad ones out…*

Common concerns are that there is no air. As with SSI say: *Look around the bubble with all your senses and you'll notice something that helps with that…*

The patient's homework is to practice bubble imagery in the supermarket or another place that feels safe or manageable for them. Each part can have a bubble, or a group one, or it can be around the whole person.

Example: A client was going to meet his new boss for the first time. He had been used to the old one and was very anxious. He put a bubble around himself before he got to work and felt it's presence. At work he reminded himself and the parts of its presence and felt more centered meeting the new boss.

Example: A client had to testify at court and was anxious. He/she put bubble armor on (i.e., a form fitting bubble) with slippery feeling-proofing. When the antagonistic defense attorney cross examined them, his harsh questions slid off the bubble.

Example: Shamus was accustomed to picking up people's projected feelings as he had been the object of his parents' projections during his childhood. His bubble helped him develop boundaries that blocked other people's projections. If he wanted to know what they were feeling, he had a valve and could let a bit in, and then send it back out.

Coping Skill: Container Imagery (Kluft, 1988)

Containers are used to store burdens that are at risk of destabilizing clients and help with stabilization during Phase 1 of trauma treatment. They are used in Phase 2 to help with managing the witnessing and unburdening process. Examples of burdens that can be stored include traumatic material the client and parts may be amnestic for, material the parts have some information about and are afraid to work on it, and feelings or beliefs that are overwhelming.

Like with SSI, developing a container or containers relies on upgrading the client's ability to dissociate. Start by noting ways the client already has an unconscious lid on traumatic or dissociated material and then assist them in upgrading it so it can be used consciously. Note: All containers have the commitment to work on everything stored inside when the time is right.

Example of Wording: *You already put lids on things that happened, like you don't have flashbacks all the time, right? Most of the time that material is stuffed behind a lid you unconsciously put on. All we're going to do is upgrade that lid and make it work better. You also lose time sometimes and don't know what happened during that time. That's another way you unconsciously block knowledge.*

Example: A client knew they had a trauma history but did not know any details and were afraid to work on it. The therapist started by saying, "*You don't know all the details of what happened. You have unconsciously been pushing that information away, dissociating it for ages. So, let's work on upgrading that unconscious lid into a container that you can use consciously, to store whatever needs to be stored. This means you will have more control and choices on when you take it out and work on it. All containers have the commitment built into them that all that's stored will be worked on when the time is right.*"

Ask questions such as: "*What kind of container would you like?*" "*What's the first image that pops in your head?*" Whatever the client's image is, work with that. If the client doesn't have an image, you can suggest something like a bank vault, a Tupperware container, or a file drawer.

Once the container is chosen, say, "*Great! Focus on the container, and as you focus on it, notice the traumatic material* (use whatever words the client uses) *is going into it in just the right way... And notice that the container gets stronger and stronger with every bit that goes into it... Let me know when the right amount is in.* (Note: This is a hypnotic linking suggestion e.g., as the material goes in, the container gets stronger and stronger.)

Once that is done, ask, "*So, what are you noticing?*" Once you get feedback from the client, say, "*That's great. And notice there's a commitment built into the container that everything stored inside it will be worked on when the time is right. Now that the material is stored, things are already changing because it isn't used to being stored in a container. So, things are already changing..."*

Example: Juanita had an extensive sex abuse history for which she was mostly amnestic. She was terrified to work on it. We identified the parts that held the information and feelings related to the sex abuse and systematically helped each part create a container. As the traumatic material was stored, the parts felt less and less anxious. Eventually, the container was used to help with the unburdening process.

Example: One client used a bank vault with safety deposit boxes stored inside the vault. Burdens were stored in different safety deposit boxes as needed, and if something came up during the week it could be stored in the vault via a night deposit box. The client began the witnessing process by choosing one safety deposit box to open.

Problem Solving Example: Carol called her therapist because her container wasn't working. The therapist asked, *"Is it a container with the commitment to work on everything when the time is right, or a container where the old stuff is pushed away forever?"* Carol said, *"The latter."* The therapist suggested she put the old stuff in a container with a commitment to work on it and call her back in 5 minutes. Carol called in 5 minutes and the material was all stored.

Problem Solving Example: Jax had a part that held rage. The part was unwilling to put the rage in a container as he thought he needed it to protect him and was afraid he'd lose the rage if it was put in a container. I explained that the part had the control, plus that having a % of the rage in the container would give him more energy to protect himself. I suggested experimenting by putting 2-5% of rage in the container and taking it out. He was still concerned he'd lose the rage. I then suggested he put a picture of a sailboat (I knew he liked sailing) inside and then take it out. As he practiced putting the picture in and taking it out, he became confident that he had control over the container. He then was willing to put two % of the rage in, then practiced putting it in and taking that out. He noticed he could breathe a bit better with the rage in, and then was willing to put seven % of the rage in for the week. I also suggested that if he wanted, he could practice taking it out and putting it back in, or he could even put more in if he wanted or take all of it out. The next session, he told me he and the parts were more relaxed during the week, and that actually he had put seventy seven % of the rage in, but he didn't want to tell me!

Example: A person had sex with their partner and experienced a wild, prolonged orgasm that felt partly great, but was also excessive and terrifying. Focusing on the feelings, they identified a little girl part who was terrified. We developed a SS for the girl, and then a container for her to put the terror in. The girl part told us she still felt funny. We identified that this part held burdens of old sexual arousal and orgasm related to deliberately being aroused during incest. Those feelings were also put in the container. The person agreed to remind the girl part to go to her SS before they had sex again. After all, children are not supposed to be present when adults have sex. Eventually the girl part was fully witnessed and unburdened.

Coping Skill: Establishing Safe Walls

One of the gifts of working with people with complex trauma disorders is that the more experience you have, the more flexible your brain becomes. I used Safe Walls in the following examples:

Example: Every time a client tried to connect with a particularly difficult exile, she found herself becoming blended. I suggested she put up a very strong protective plexiglass wall between her and the exile. The wall did not help, until she realized she needed to put her hands on the wall and feel the cool, strong surface of it. Then she could stay unblended and interact with the exile.

Example: During witnessing of one target, a client realized there were a number of parts present that were unknown. Because of the risk of these parts becoming overwhelmed by the traumatic material, a safe place was established around the unknown parts. Because we weren't sure that worked, we put a safe wall around the parts involved in the witnessing just to be sure. The safe wall contained feeling and soundproofing. The target was successfully witnessed, and unburdened.

Coping Skill: Affect Dial (Brown and Fromm, 1986)

Affect dials are basically like dimmer switches for lights or volume controls for televisions and are used for controlling the intensity of feelings. They help clients to remain in control of their emotions. I suggest putting a SUDs (subjective units of distress) scale on it with zero being no feelings and 10 being the strongest. This is an example of how I taught it, to an adult part:

> *You know what a dimmer switch is, right? So, picture a dimmer switch with a SUDs scale on it. What's something that happened this week that was irritating, you know like forgetting to buy cat food and having to go shopping in the rain... What number is it on the dimmer switch?... A 3? Ok. Now focus on the 3 "pissed off" feeling on the dimmer switch... Notice how that feels... And turn the dial up to a 4... What do you notice?... Now turn it back down to a 3 and notice the changes... And turn it down to a 2... What's that like?... Now turn it off... and back on...and now dial it up to a 7... And now back down to a 5...to a 2...turn it off, and back on...What's that like?... Good going. You're doing great learning to have control of feelings.*

After this is learned and practiced, we work on using the dimmer switch on something that's a higher SUDs level. The client is asked to practice this during the week and to help other parts learn and practice it.

Two principals help with this process:

1. If you focus on a negative feeling like anger or pain, you begin to feel worse. As it's generally easier to feel worse than better, you first ask the client to turn the dial up to feel a little more anger or pain. This gives the client confidence because if they can turn it up, they can turn it down!
2. The client has the ability to block things out, dissociate or numb, so again, you are upgrading the client's ability from all or nothing, to levels in between. Note: This skill can be also taught by starting with a positive feeling and turning it up and down.

Example: A client was arguing with her husband and felt out of control. She turned her anger from an 8 down to a 4, felt more in control and could continue the argument.

Example: A woman was anxious about a plumber coming. She reminded child parts to go to their safe spaces and put sound- and feeling-proofing up. She then used the affect dial to dial down her own anxiety until she felt okay about the man coming to repair the sink.

Coping Skill: Deep Dreamless Healing Sleep or Therapeutic Sleep (Kluft, 1988)

This is a coping skill that is easy for many parts to learn. As with SSI, I ask one part to volunteer to try it out and ask all others who are willing to watch to learn how to do it. Once a part volunteers, I speak with that part, or I work with that part through an older part with some Self energy. Deep dreamless sleep provides parts with a deep rest without nightmares, useful because so many of these clients have trouble sleeping. In this example a child part has volunteered to try it, and the example provides suggestions for wording. It begins with me talking directly to the child part.

> *Hi, thanks for volunteering. Do you have any questions or concerns right now, or is it okay to go to your safe space?... Great, look around and notice everything there that makes it safe, and that there's a comfortable place to rest, where you can relax, as you start feeling sleepy...First I'm going to explain what we're going to do and if you've got any questions, let me know. I'm going to count backwards from 10 to 1, and as I count, you'll fall gently asleep, and by the time I reach 1 you'll be in a deep dreamless healing sleep. I'll watch the clock, and when 5 minutes is up, you can wake up—actually, if you want to wake up sooner, that's ok too, or the other parts can wake you up. Is that ok? Great... so, 10...9 feeling comfortable and sleepy...at 8 and 7... gently sleeping....at 6 and 5 in a deep dreamless sleep... and going deeper and deeper at 4 and 3... at 2...and 1 in a deep dreamless healing sleep.....*

Then, orient to the other parts and check in with them: *While this part is sleeping, I'd like to check in with the rest of you. First, how does she look?... What's this like for you having her asleep? Any questions? Any other comments?...*

Note: I watch the clock carefully for whatever time we've agreed on.

Okay, 5 minutes is up right now, is she awake yet? No? Okay, could one of you wake her up... I prefer to have the parts take control and wake her. Then I address the part: *So what was that like for you?*

Example: A client planned to visit her parents. 3 parts were terrified. They agreed to sleep through the visit, which helped the client manage the visit with less agitation.

Example: One woman had been hospitalized every May for seven years. We identified a group of 50 baby parts who got triggered in May. They didn't want to be hospitalized again and agreed to sleep from the end of April to the beginning of June. We went through the deep dreamless sleep process and then, when they were deeply asleep added: *You'll have all the time you need to feel rested and relaxed and although calendar time will be passing it will feel like only a short amount of time has passed...* This is a time when I forgot to ask if any other parts had concerns. Two days later, I got a call from a terrified teenage part whose job was to babysit the babies. She calmed down when I explained where they were. The next session, she and several other teen parts asked if they could also sleep through May. Of note, the client made it through May without hospitalization. She also realized that having the baby and teen parts asleep meant she suddenly had to do all of the "boring" filing at work. She had not been aware that they had been taking care of this for her. Note the use of the hypnotic dynamic of Time Distortion.

Conclusion

This chapter plus consultation and further training when needed will help you begin to integrate hypnotic language and coping skills in the treatment of this population and others. A variety of skills have been presented as not everything works for everyone, and hopefully, the variety will assist you in adapting these skills and/or developing others as clients' individual needs dictate. Clients benefit from having their dissociative symptoms upgraded into coping skills. This protects clients from decompensating and helps them to manage their symptoms and maintain the highest level of functioning during their healing process.

> Note: Some therapists come to consultations with saying, "*My client is doing great. She's dissociating less.*" As this is not a sign of progress unless the client is in the last stages of treatment, I respond, "*What you really want is for them to be dissociating better!*"

CHAPTER 5

Accessing for and Diagnosing Dissociative Disorders

Introduction: IFS and Diagnosis: To Diagnosis or Not

IFS views diagnosis and the DSM as a way of describing parts that are burdened and activated, and as pathologizing (Anderson et al. 2017). It is not good clinical practice when clinicians use diagnosis or the DSM to pathologize, pathologize in general and/or take a diagnosis as rigid truth. I prefer to think of diagnosis as a quick way of describing symptom patterns and, as the Diagnostic and Statistical Manual IV (2013) states, the "DSM is intended to serve as a practical, functional, and flexible guide for organizing information that can aid in the accurate diagnosis and treatment of mental disorders." Translating symptoms of DSM diagnoses into parts is a useful way of identifying parts that are present and allows one to hypothesize the existence of others. Not everyone will meet every criterion for diagnosis but checking for and/or ruling out potential symptoms helps make treatment more comprehensive.

Familiarity with the various presentations of dissociation, knowing how to recognize dissociative symptoms and the ability to initiate diagnostic testing when needed is important. Seven studies of DID clients show that on the average they have spent between 7–11.9 years in treatment prior to diagnosis (ISSTD Treatment Guidelines 2011) and receiving adequate treatment. Clinical studies in the US and abroad found that up to 20 % of patients in general and specialty inpatient psychiatric units, meet DSM-IV-TR (American Psychiatric Association 2000) diagnostic criteria for DID, and that many more meet the criteria for Other Specified Dissociative Disorder (OSDD).

Underdiagnosis or delay in diagnosis is common as the dynamics of dissociation involves hiding information internally from oneself, as well as interpersonally. Diagnosis and identification of dissociative symptoms and disorders leads to a wealth of references and resources on safe, successful, efficient treatment in addition to the information in this book.

How Clients with Dissociative Disorders Present

People with dissociative disorders initially present with all the usual treatment issues. Sometimes they know they have a dissociative disorder and are waiting for you to ask the right questions, so they know you are receptive, knowledgeable, and not judgmental. Some have no idea they have a dissociative disorder. Some of them will have lives that are functional and stable, while others may be overtly dysfunctional and leading chaotic lives. Regardless of their presentation, along with the other assessment steps that you may take, keep in mind the symptoms signaling the possibility of dissociative disorders and evaluate over time.

Here are some examples of the initial presentations of clients who spent many years in treatment with respected therapists before being diagnosed with DID:

- A human resource professional who needed help socializing at work.

Accessing for and Diagnosing Dissociative Disorders

- A carpenter with anxiety who had frequent minor accidents.
- A mother of two who wanted to stop "wasting time" playing video games.
- A woman who needed to quit smoking after having several bronchitis attacks.
- A man in the middle of a master's program in classical piano.

Two of these people had very strong dissociative systems and strong managers and were lucky enough to not have anything trigger their exiles to the point where their systems became overwhelmed. The other three were less lucky. Their treatment overwhelmed managers, and unleashed raging firefighters. They lost careers, relationships, stability, and years of their lives to self-destructive behaviors and misery. All of them spent considerable amounts of money on treatment that was not adequate and three ended up on long term disability. All were easily diagnosed with DID or OSDD and, once on the correct treatment path, began making the progress they could have made years earlier.

There are many pathways to misdiagnosis, for example, typical batteries of psychological testing do not include testing for dissociative disorders and clinicians giving them rarely know what to look for to accurately diagnosis dissociative disorders. Additionally, trauma disorders are at times overshadowed by symptoms that fit into another diagnosis with overlapping symptomology. Eighty % of Schneiderian symptoms used to diagnose schizophrenia are related to dissociation, and many people diagnosed with ADHD have untreated trauma disorders. Borderline personality disorder is a trauma disorder which is high on the dissociation continuum. Bipolar disorder is sometimes diagnosed when a person has different presentations (depressed part, manic part) during the same session or across time. It is said that if a person only has a hammer, all their problems are seen as nails. Restated, if a psychiatrist or therapist doesn't know what to look for, they will "never" see anyone with a dissociative disorder. Note: there are times when dual diagnosis is appropriate, e.g., clients can have schizophrenia and a dissociative disorder or may have major depression and C-PTSD. Therefore, it is important to continue to assess the client while considering the possibility that a diagnosis could be more representative of symptoms that may disappear once traumatic material has been dealt with.

Suggestive Signs and Symptoms of DID, and OSDD

Diagnosis of persons with DID and OSDD is often not difficult if you know what to look for and are aware of the signs. As one IFS therapist said, *"When I first started learning about dissociative disorders, I didn't get it. And then it was like scales fell from my eyes, and now when it's there, I see it."* Diagnosis is simply a matter of learning what to look for, knowing what questions to ask, listening to and observing how answers are given, along with persistent curiosity and openness. It is also important to appreciate that some clients with an inner system or intuition of dissociative parts will seek out IFS treatment because of IFS's belief in normal multiplicity and its parts model. They may know they need to work with parts, and not know how dissociated their parts are.

Table 1 provides a list of what to look for during initial sessions. When one or more of these "Suggestive Signs" are noticed, take steps to clarify or rule out the presence of dissociative symptoms and diagnosis. Given that anyone with a dissociative disorder has grown up needing to hide from others and from themselves, the information needed for diagnosis initially may be unavailable. Diagnosis needs to be evaluated and reevaluated over time as you and your client work together.

A list of Suggestive Signs of Dissociative Disorders, Kluft (1999, 9), Lyons-Ruth (2001), Brown, Steinberg (2000), Twombly (2005)

1. Prior treatment failure(s).
2. Three or more prior diagnoses.
3. Concurrent psychiatric and somatic symptoms.
4. Fluctuating symptoms and levels of functioning.
5. Severe headaches (occur in over 80% of DD clients) and other pain syndromes.
6. Time distortion, time lapses, or frank amnesia.
7. Being told of disremembered behaviors.
8. Others noting observable changes.
9. The discovery of objects, productions, or handwriting in one's possession that one cannot account for or recognize.

10. Hearing voices (80% or more experienced as within the head) that are experienced as separate, often urging the client toward some activity.
11. The client's use of "we" in a collective sense and/or making self-referential statements in the third person.
12. The eliciting of other entities through hypnosis or IFS.
13. A history of child abuse.
14. An inability to recall childhood events from the years 6-11.
15. History of early neglect, abandonment, parents with attachment disorders.
16. Disorganized attachment.
17. Countertransference feelings of spaciness, being dissociated or less articulate than usual. Note: Tracking one's countertransference is always important and is key with clients who, by virtue of threats and dissociation, may nonverbally communicate something about being dissociative.

    Example 1: I was meeting with a new client and realized I was feeling dizzy and a little disconnected. I recognized that she might have a dissociative disorder. This was later confirmed.

    Example 2: I felt dizzy with a client and then later realized I was sick. It is always important to stay open and curious about the source of feelings.

18. Client with many symptoms who report they had a "great childhood."
19. Psychogenic or pseudo seizures (seizures that happen without any physical reason).
20. 5 dimensions of dissociation (Steinberg, 2000):
    1. Amnesia: Loss of time, loss of awareness of periods of time in the past or present.

Accessing for and Diagnosing Dissociative Disorders

>   2. Depersonalization: Not feeling attached to oneself or a part of oneself, or a sense of not being real.
>   3. Derealization: Not feeling attached to one's environment.
>   4. Identity confusion: Not knowing who you are.
>   5. Identity alteration: A sense of having parts that are more separate than regular IFS parts.

21. Therapists working with the refuge/immigrant population, and people who have grown up during wars or dangerous circumstances (i.e., organized crime families and areas with ongoing gang violence) also need to be aware that early ongoing violence can result in the development of dissociative disorders, especially if a person's life was further complicated by a difficult family of origin, major losses, abandonment, etc.
22. A client who reports having a *"good childhood"* but has many symptoms.

Aside from being aware of suggestive symptoms of a possible dissociative disorder, it is a simple matter to weave a few questions from the Dissociative Experience Scale (Bernstein and Putnam, 1986) and other tests into initial sessions. These are examples of a few questions I've adapted from the DES taxon, the 8 questions out of the 28 DES questions that are most applicable to the diagnosis of DID.:

- *"Do you ever have the feeling that your body doesn't belong to you?"*
- *"Do you ever have the sense that something happened to you and you're not sure if it really happened or not?"*
- *"Does it sometimes seem like there are voices in your head telling you things or arguing?"*

- "Do you ever feel like you're a little kid trying to handle adult things?"

As you ask these questions and/or use a diagnostic test, notice how your client answers. Hesitations, confusion, pauses, eyelids fluttering or rolling up, or answering very quickly can be indications of parts interacting or arguing. It can help to ask, *"When I asked that question, you looked like you were really thinking about how to answer it. What was going on in your head?"* As always, gentle curiosity is helpful.

Sometimes diagnosis is extremely easy, and some clients feel relief when questions about dissociative symptoms are asked and parts are identified. Other times, exposing the existence of parts may stir up panic because secrecy enabled their survival. Watch for this as the identification and discussion of parts may need to be handled carefully and gradually.

Example: A client came in for a first session. IFS, normal multiplicity, and working with parts was discussed. The client appeared interested but never returned. Some months later the same person came into treatment with me. She was anxious and hesitant around identifying parts and eventually stated, *"If you know about them* (the parts), *I'm going to die."*

Diagnostic Tests and Questionnaires

As mentioned above, standard batteries of psychological tests largely leave out questions about dissociative symptoms and are not helpful with diagnosis unless the test administrator specifically knows what to look for. Diagnostic tests and questionnaires that adequately assist with diagnosing dissociative disorders can be easy to give, and many are available online. See the appendix for web URL sources. These tests and questionnaires offer good reliability and validity.

The Somatoform Dissociation Questionnaire (SDQ) (5 and 20) was developed by Nijenhuis in 1996 and diagnoses the client through questions about somatoform symptoms of dissociation, e.g., pain when urinating and areas of numbness in the body. This test is particularly useful for people who have symptoms that express themselves more somatically than not. It is also useful to give the SDQ or ask questions from it, as these questions introduce the somatic dimension and address areas that clients may feel too much shame about to discuss. Additionally, they may believe such experiences are normal because they have lived with them for so long. For example, a person whose pelvic area has always been numb will not recognize that that is not typical.

The Dissociative Experience Scale II (DES) (Bernstein and Putnam, 1986) has 28 questions and is also easy to give. It is available in different versions for both adolescents and children. Again, administering these questionnaires in session gives you a chance to observe the client's response.

Example: One client, barely taking time to hear the whole question answered *"No"* to all questions. When I asked what was happening inside her as I asked the questions, she quickly answered *"Nothing."* Treatment went very slowly until we identified parts of her who refused to allow other parts answer any questions.

Example: A client answered questions extremely slowly, stumbling over words and looking lost. When I asked what was happening inside her she said, *"No one is supposed to know anything. It's like there's a battle going on inside me."*

Clients with parts who refuse to answer questions and clients with more dissociative internal systems of parts may end up with false negative results on diagnostic testing. One example of this was a client who had no awareness of parts. Once the parts began interacting with me they said, *"She doesn't know anything about us."* Another client appeared comfortable answering DES questions and got a low score. Three months later, she began describing dissociative symptoms using some of the wording from the DES. She later explained that parts were afraid I would think she was crazy and kick her out of treatment if she answered questions honestly.

To clarify, low test scores may mean the client is not on the dissociative spectrum. On the other hand, it may mean the client, for whatever reason, is hiding or unaware of the correct answers. Diagnosis is a process and may need to occur over a lengthy period of time.

Shame is another reason why clients may not answer accurately. In many places mental health issues carry a stigma, especially for those living with DID who have symptoms that, without context, can appear strange. This can occur even in the IFS community, which is generally non-pathologizing and compassionate. For example , one very experienced IFS therapist described DID clients, as clients with parts who …"continually lie, hide, and distort the truth…" While this may be symptomatically true for some clients, it does not carry the compassionate reality of how these behaviors might have been necessary in order to minimize abuse and maintain attachment, and which over time, become unconsciously habitual. It is always important to ask, *"What concerns do you have about telling me the truth?"* and to realize that overcoming knowledge programed and beaten into a client takes time. It is important for therapists to be open, nonjudgemental, persistent, and aware of the dynamics in these very complicated families.

Example: One client said, *"I was so afraid, I lied all the time and sometimes it got me out of beatings. I lied so much I sometimes forgot what was true, and even now I catch myself lying when I don't have to."* I told her, *"Of course you had to lie. Your parents punished you for telling the truth and there was so much abuse, I would think you would have done anything to avoid it. It makes sense to me that you still catch yourself lying sometimes. When you notice you've lied to me,* *just let me know so we can understand what triggered it. Maybe it will be because you weren't ready to tell me something, maybe it will be out of habit, maybe it will be because you or parts of you were triggered, or maybe something else. It's just a symptom of coming from a very difficult family."*

More complex and comprehensive diagnostics include:

- The Structured Clinical Interview for Dissociative disorders (SCID-D) (Steinberg, 1995, 2004).
- The Multidimensional Inventory of Dissociation (MID) (Dell, 2006). The adult MID is available in several different languages. The adolescent MID is only available in English.

More information can be obtained by reading Brand, B. & Armstrong, J. & Loewenstein, R. (2006). Psychological Assessment of Patients with Dissociative Identity Disorders.

Examples of indications that a client might be on the dissociative spectrum include:

"I've been to the ER with chest pains five times and the stupid doctors say nothing's wrong with me."

"My husband says I did such and such. He's a total liar." Or, *"My spouse complains I never listen to her."*

"Sorry I forgot to come in last week." (Client was there!)

"I can't remember anything we talked about last week."

"I have a terrible memory."

"I get so anxious at work; I can't remember how to do half the stuff I'm supposed to."

"I found these cute boots in my closet, and I can't remember buying them. I finally decided I was going to wear them because they're really comfortable."

"I never use Novocain when I go to the dentist. I don't need to; I have a high pain tolerance."

"I know where my home is, it doesn't feel like mine."

"I have a great life, but I'm always anxious. I never feel safe."

"I don't have any parts."

When Self is described, the client says, *"nothing is there"* or *"nothing is inside."*

Summary

Diagnosis is something that may be easy to determine or may need to be clarified over time. Once diagnosed, you may decide to not share it with the client especially if the client is phobic of the disorder. In this case, being an IFS therapist is an advantage since diagnosis is not recommended, and because of IFS's belief in normal multiplicity. One option is to say, *"We're just doing IFS therapy with coping skills built-in."* If a client asks about their diagnosis I often comment, *"It's the normal result of an abnormal childhood. How else could you have gotten through your childhood and maintained the ability to care about people and heal."* What is of particular importance is to know when a client has dissociated parts, as these clients will either require Trauma Informed IFS or at the very least benefit from it.

Most of my clients know they have DID or OSDD and this has helped them make sense of their symptoms. In addition, it has allowed them to access resources on dissociative disorders that have helped them move forward versus staying stuck.

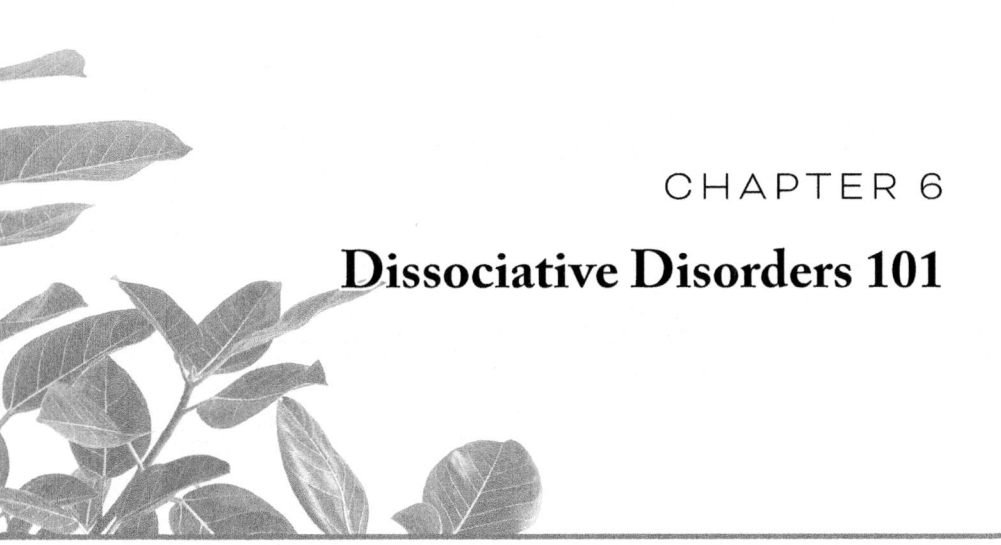

CHAPTER 6

Dissociative Disorders 101

Introduction

Dissociative symptoms occur in most, and perhaps all, clients who experienced early relational, physical, or sexual trauma and neglect. Untreated dissociative symptoms and disorders slow down, prevent, and/or complicate treatment. The DSM-5 states that dissociation is a failure to integrate aspects of identity, memory, perception, and consciousness. Another definition is "fright without solution (Lyons- Ruth, 2001)", a chilling reality for children trapped in these difficult families.

This book will focus on the most common dissociative disorders including Dissociative Identity Disorder (DID), Other Specified Dissociative Disorder (OSDD), and Complex-Post Traumatic Stress Disorder (C-PTSD). Please note that OSDD is like DID but does not include the criteria for amnesia or more than one part taking over executive control. This section provides a brief review of DID and dissociation, in general.

> **DSM-5 criteria for DID requires:**
>
> 1. Switching between two or more alters (parts)
> 2. Recurrent amnesia between alters
> 3. Symptoms causing distress or dysfunction
> 4. Symptoms not due to culture, religion, or fantasy
> 5. Symptoms not due to substance abuse or another condition

Many disorders have dissociative symptoms including eating disorders, addictions, OCD, ADHD, depression, and anxiety disorders. Because of this, it is always helpful to rule in or out the possibility that these clients may have a dissociative disorder. You will find that many of the strategies in this book will help clients with general and specific trauma and dissociative disorders.

Etiology

Dissociative disorders were originally thought of as trauma disorders. More recent research by Lyons-Ruth (2001) indicates that dissociative symptoms also develop in people who as infants, experienced neglect, exhibited signs of disorganized attachment, and/or had primary caretakers who were physically unavailable during the first two years of their life. Research also shows that infants who exhibit disorganized attachment, develop it in relation to parents who are "frightened or frightening" (Liotti, 1999). Abuse frequently occurs in these kinds of families which necessitates further dissociation. These families are also the ones who tend to not notice when their child(ren) is/are being abused by a neighbor or other persons. Clinically it is important to realize, that along with abuse, there is a foundation of neglect and attachment disorders which also need to be treated.

Are DID Clients Different from Everyone Else?

The concept of normal multiplicity is well known to IFS therapists and to ego state therapists. Clients with complex dissociative disorders are not different from anyone else, but their systems are more complex, their parts are more dissociated, and they carry more extreme burdens. Thus, they are at an increased risk of becoming overwhelmed and destabilized. The symptom manifestation and nonverbal communication inherent in treating these clients may additionally challenge the internal system of the therapist.

In this diagram you can see a representation of the thickness of boundaries around parts of the mind. "Normal" ego states or parts have thinner walls that allow for a flow of communication among parts and Self. The word "pathology" in the diagram is used as a description of a condition that causes symptomatic behavior for the person once they are an adult. There is no negative connotation. It is not a choice or a matter of survival ability.

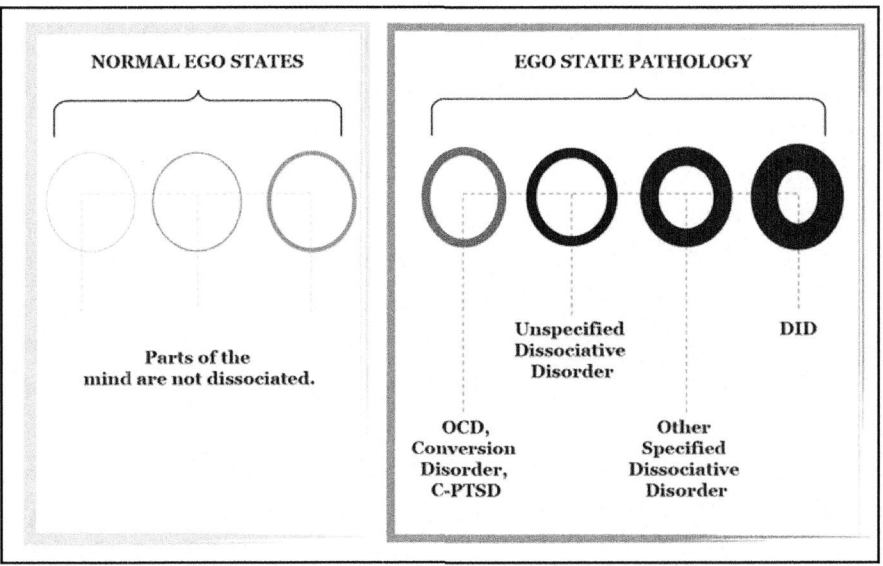

People with DID have lived through childhoods requiring extreme survival strategies to manage physical, emotional, and/or sexual trauma, neglect, and parenting by attachment disordered parents. The very strategies needed for survival become problematic and limit the client's functioning once they have grown up and moved away from their families. Like veterans who have difficulty adapting to living in a non-combat situation, people with DID have the skills to exist in highly traumatic circumstances. These skills however, make it difficult to function in the world as it is today. Managers, firefighters, and exiles are organized around keeping often volcanic traumatic burdens under a lid or contained in some manner.

Two things make this impossible over our lifetimes: One, we are biologically wired to heal both physically and emotionally, which means there is a healing force that is pushing against whatever management strategies a person uses to push away the impact of trauma. And two, management strategies use up energy and managers get depleted over time. An analogy I tell clients who are wondering why they can't push traumatic material away like they used to is: *"It's like peeing. You can hold it back for a while, but eventually it begins to seep out and then it gushes."*

Ultimately, a goal is to help clients access Self. These clients tend to have a difficult time getting into Self, because they grew up in families where being in Self or showing Self energy was dangerous. Clients may find it necessary to block out any hope, confidence, achievement, and positive self-esteem, and may need to align themselves with the beliefs of their parents, i.e., "I'm *bad. I'm stupid. I'm good for nothing."* etc.

To maintain attachment to parents, abuse must be dissociated or blamed on oneself or a part(s). Normal feelings and motivations verbally or nonverbally can get twisted into making the child blame him/herself. "I loved Daddy, it felt good, I wanted it, I asked him to…" *"Identifying with abusers' ideologies and motivations not only sustains attachment possibilities, but allows victims to endure excruciating, otherwise intolerable guilt and shame.*" (Schwartz, H. 2000)

I think of it as a desperate if you can't beat them join them necessity. "*Where there should be an internalized benevolent parent... there is instead, the internalized offender, with his harsh, blaming, judgmental, and occasionally sadistic attacks. Incapable of self-soothing, the victim turns to distraction instead, and works, drinks, drugs, sexualized, clings, rails, or simply makes endless lists in her too busy life.*" (Salter 1995)

In one of my IFS trainings, Richard Schwartz talked about abusive parents not liking it when their children are in Self. They have their own agendas and can get triggered when their children are proud, happy, confident, or achieving something. Self energy is thus, something to be avoided. In addition, parents can have untreated dissociative disorders, and the child must adjust to different parts of the parents. One boy's mother had a "good Mom" part, a part who hated boys, and a sadistic part who liked to hurt her children. He grew up with a part who loved his mom and learned positive skills from her, a part who acted effeminate, and a part who cowered and held the terror of the mother's sadistic part. Client examples of times when parents punished Self energy follow:

Example: One boy was required to get all As but if anyone outside of the family praised him his mother got enraged and punished him.

Example: One girl was home alone practicing her clarinet when her father came home, grabbed the clarinet, and smashed it.

Example: Three siblings were laughing together. Their father came down from upstairs, hit two of them, and left the third to clean up the kitchen.

Direct Access

It makes sense that children in these circumstances learn to avoid and fear Self energy. Because of this, most of the early work with people with Complex PTSD and people with dissociative disorders will need to be done through direct access. Discussion of Self often needs to be put off or therapists will run the risk of confusing their clients or giving them an impossible task.

It is however, important for the therapist to be in Self most of the time. I visualize connecting my Self energy with the Self of the client, and the Self energy of all the parts.

One good description of the internal world and external presentation of clients with an overt DID presentation follows: The patient experiences "... *switching of personalities, the dissociative and amnestic barriers, and the complexity of internal psychic structures and identity"...*" *periodic intrusions of re-experiencing phenomena, including flashbacks, nightmares, overwhelming affect, and even somatic sensations lend a sense of chronic instability" ...(combined with)* "*comorbid characterological difficulties including patients' intense interpersonal disturbances, affective instability, and impulsive and self-destructive behavior" (which all) "add to the sense of ongoing crisis and chaos."* Chu, J. (1998). I chose to quote this as it is a vivid and compelling description of what these clients live with.

Some people with dissociative disorders are living chaotic lives and some are extremely high-functioning with many ego strengths. High-functioning people with dissociative disorders may be teachers, therapists, psychiatrists, lawyers, parents, etc. Their existence can appear solid if their dissociative boundaries have not been breached. They are, however, also at risk for destabilization if their need for stabilization skills is not recognized. It is important for these clients to develop coping skills before working on trauma material or witnessing, so they can have the ability to continue to be at their highest level of functioning.

Another high-functioning DID pattern is exemplified by clients with an overtly competent façade who need to look good (which could be the result of intense shame about having symptoms). This can easily distract therapists from exploring the underlying reasons for symptoms. This can lead to superficial treatment with a therapist the client likes and respects, while feeling more and more shame for not making progress. As therapists rarely take responsibility for what they do not know, this reinforces the common childhood belief that there is something essentially wrong with the client, and lack of progress in treatment is proof.

Differences Between Standard IFS and Trauma and Dissociation Informed IFS

IFS describes parts as "discrete, autonomous mental systems, each with their own idiosyncratic range of emotion, style of expression, abilities, desires and views of the world." (Schwartz, R. Sweezy, M. 2020) and they're categorized as Managers, Firefighters, and Exiles. Managers and Firefighters are considered the parts with jobs, who are protective. Exiles are considered parts who carry burdens and do not have jobs. Trauma Informed IFS regards Exiles as also having jobs, in that they carry the majority of the burdens, thus freeing up other parts to function in different ways. They often feel and appear weak, but their ability to carry burdens for years requires strength and energy. Once unburdened, their strength will be available to the whole system. Sisyphus was an exile who no one would consider as weak!

Parts for people with dissociative disorders are generally more complicated, disconnected and are more polarized from each other than regular IFS parts. This makes sense, as they were developed in relation to more complicated circumstances. Aside from parts frequently seen in standard IFS, examples of parts and the possible need for these parts include:

- Parts with no bodies: if you have no body, you can't be hurt.
- Opposite sex parts/sexless parts: if I was a boy (or a girl or an it) I wouldn't have been abused.
- Fragments: A part's only existence consisted of a memory of her father making her scrambled eggs. This positive memory maintained attachment.
- Malevolent, perpetrator-identified parts.
- Positive introjects of fantasized, real people or book characters.
- Parts who hide other parts, blank things out.
- Numb, deaf, paralyzed and/or blind parts
- A part who's only purpose is to have sex: if you're being sexually abused every night, it is helpful to have a part who "likes it" and easily lubricates or gets an erection.
- Robot (no feelings), a rock (can't be hurt), etc.

Another reality of working with DID and DDNOS is to remember that they live with what Kluft (1993) called "multiple reality disorder" and described as living in *"... several parallel but incompletely overlapping constructions of the world and of life experience."* In practice, therapists must remember that, one, the part of the DID person who shows up for treatment and seems like a whole person, is not. Two, parts not addressed directly frequently are not listening and probably won't be learning whatever you're teaching, and three, that many parts will be stuck in the past, i.e., believing they are still children, living where they grew up, with their parents, and being abused every day.

People with dissociative disorders who are lucky enough to come into treatment with intact dissociative symptoms often function quite well and can be relatively stable. I think of these systems as like a stable house of cards. When that stability is breached without adequate coping skills, the traumatic material rushes out and treatment becomes excessively complicated. When this happens, clients are forced to become excessively dependent on the therapist as their source of self-soothing and reassurance, and on more extreme ways of managing their symptoms, e.g., drinking excessively, increased self-destructive behavior and suicidality. Another analogy is a house built with strong appearing beams that are riddled with termite damage. Harry Belafonte sang about this in his song, Hosana. *"House built on a weak foundation, Will not stand, oh no…"*

Two Important Final Notes

One question that is frequently asked is whether the goal of treatment is integration or integrated functioning. There is no right or wrong here, as trauma therapists have been comprehensively healing people with complex trauma and dissociative disorders for years without the benefit of IFS. My IFS training has evolved my concept of healing in that I now think that as healing occurs, the client's internal system integrates and reconfigures into a healthy Self-led system. Although IFS teaches that no parts get lost, with complex DID clients it is a little different in at least a couple ways.

1. Parts who are fragments benefit from integrating with other parts so they can heal and have a more complete experience of life.

    Example: One woman had a part who only screamed, another who only scratched her face until it was bleeding, and one who only felt pain. To witness these parts it was necessary to temporarily merge them with a part who could think. Once these parts were witnessed and unburdened they integrated into one stronger part.
2. Groups of parts within clients with complex systems may integrate as trauma gets witnessed and unburdened.

Example: A client with a very complex system had a group of 50 baby parts cared for by a caretaker part. Once their trauma was processed, they spontaneously integrated into one. The one resulting part reported that she felt stronger and more capable. She had a sense that all the parts were there in a different way and nothing was lost.

Conclusion

This section is a very quick overview of DID and dissociation in general. Additional information is provided in other sections and chapters, and resources for more learning are available in the appendix.

CHAPTER 7
Complex PTSD 101

The diagnosis Complex PTSD was recognized in the International Classification of Disease 11 (ICD 11) in 2018. It was first proposed in 1992 by Judith Herman in her pivotal book "*Trauma and Recovery*" *1997*. Herman identified six symptom groups which continue to be hallmarks of C-PTSD: disturbance of affect regulation, alterations of consciousness, disturbed self-perception, disturbed perception of the offender, relationship problems, and changes in the value system. In spite of continued advocacy, C-PTSD has not been included in the DSM, although a new category which comes close, PTSD Dissociative Subtype was added to the DSM 5 in 2013. To meet the criteria for PTSD Dissociative Subtype, one has to meet the diagnostic criteria for PTSD plus dissociative symptoms, derealization and/or depersonalization.

Clinical observation and research have linked C-PTSD with multiple traumatic events during childhood and/or adulthood, interpersonal victimization, and extended periods of traumatic exposure. (Luxenberg, 2001). Ford (2017) listed the following five "I's" of complex trauma: "*Intentional interpersonal acts that are inescapable and cause injury that is potentially irreparable*", and in his book with Courtois (2020) *Treating Complex Traumatic Stress*

Disorders in Adults, more "I's" were added: *"complex traumatic stressors are highly intimate, intrusive, and invasive of the body and the self of the individual, often involving imminent threat, the totality of which results in deformations of identity and disrupting interpersonal capacity for intimate and other relationships."*

Recommended treatment includes emotion regulation, cognitive re-appraisal and self-compassion. (Lanius, 2019. Luxenberg, 2001), within the three phases of phase-oriented treatment (Ford and Courtois, 2020). While clients with C-PTSD are often less complicated to treat than clients with dissociative disorders, the same risk factors of decreased functioning and decompensation exist if treatment overwhelms the clients' ability to cope. Many of the coping skills in this book can be used with these clients.

CHAPTER 8

Memory

Memory and Therapeutic Neutrality

When treating clients, it is important to understand that "memory" is not always accurate. It is impacted by many factors, including age at time of event, other peoples' retelling of history (or perhaps lying), family messages, programing, the need to keep secrets, drug and alcohol use, and dissociation. We therapists were not present during our clients' childhoods; therefore, we cannot validate that they were traumatized, just as we cannot validate that they were not traumatized. Because memory is not always accurate, I call "memories" traumatic material. As they are processed, our clients can decide what makes sense about their history, and/or live with the peace that comes with healing.

Example: One child desperately needed to tell someone that she was being sexually abused, but was too afraid to tell on her father, a violent perpetrator who had threated to beat her if she told. Instead, she reported that a favorite teacher had molested her, perhaps because he was a safe man who would not punish or abuse her for telling. She was believed at face value. He was fired, and it was months before the actual truth was discovered.

Example: A young woman with close ties to her family came into treatment with detailed knowledge of being abused in a cult. Eventually, it became clear that her father had sadistically abused her, while her mother, who knew about the abuse, assured the client she was loved, and that everyone outside the family would hurt her. The cult abuse memories evaporated during treatment and appeared to be the result of contagion factor from a hospitalization where she heard many abuse details from other patients. The vivid cult "memories" filled in amnestic periods of the client's life and became a screen protecting her from the worse pain of knowing her family had abused her.

Example: A man reported that he had been raped by many different men. After some trauma work, the total number of perpetrators was reduced. Several parts had different memories of being raped and did not realize that some of the rapists were the same few men seen through the eyes of different parts.

Example: A woman came into treatment because of her history of sex abuse. She had many symptoms of having had a sex abuse history, and a previous therapist had concluded that she had one. This information felt right to the client who was amnestic for large amounts of her childhood. After much work, it became clear to her that she had learned her "sex abuse" symptoms from her mother who had been sexually abused by her own father. There was physical and emotional abuse during the client's childhood, not sex abuse.

Example: A client reported that she was crazy, over sensitive, and a liar, and that her family was warm and loving. Her beliefs were based on what she had been told by her parents.

Example: A client reported that she had terrible hallucinations, and that she was a horrible person for having these bad thoughts. Our initial treatment plan was to heal the pain and horror she experienced during the "hallucinations", so she could have them without the accompanying distress. Eventually, she got corroboration from her father that her great uncle had raped both his sister who died in her teens, possibly of suicide, and her when she was around four. He told her that her uncle had loved her and that it was Christian "to turn the other cheek ."

Recommendations

Courtois (1999) summarizes the following recommendations for managing client "memories" and/or reported traumatic material.

1. The therapist strives to practice from a neutral perspective regarding memory.
2. The therapist understands the malleability of human memory and the differences between historical and narrative truth.
3. The therapist's goal in attending to traumatic memories is to facilitate mastery and resolution.

When a client asks, "Do you believe me?" it is very tempting to simply say, "I believe you." In the short term, a client may find this reassuring, but it validates something that might not be true, and possibly slows down treatment by adding another layer to an already complicated treatment. A recommendation is to explain memory dynamics and say, *"We need to spread everything out on the table and eventually you will be able to figure out what makes sense about your history."*

CHAPTER 9

Medication

Introduction

The purpose of competent use of psychiatric medication is not to "control or banish" parts, as indicated by Schwartz (2013). Like a cast provides external support allowing a broken leg the time and support for healing, medication can be thought of as an internal cast, allowing a traumatized brain and body the time and support it needs for healing. Kluft (1998) wrote, when someone has DID every effort should be made to minimize the pain of their life and painful treatment process. I tell clients, *"There are side effects to taking medication, but there are also side effects to not taking it."* The physical, emotional, and sometimes social side effects of not taking medication can be enormous. For some clients, being on medication makes working, staying out of the hospital, and functioning possible. Medication may also ease or make possible progress in treatment.

Reasons and Uses for Medication

The purpose of competent use of psychiatric medication is to give parts more control, by assisting them in dealing with symptoms. Possible uses of medication include:

- Use of medication in the beginning of treatment to take the edge off symptoms while the client is learning coping and stabilization skills.
- Use of medication long term to ease the treatment process and help the client function at their highest level possible.
- Use of PRN's (medication taken as needed) to help with extreme symptoms including flashbacks, backlash, anxiety, and panic attacks, and or as a cushion or added protection during the witnessing of particularly difficult traumatic material.
- Use of PRNs to assist clients with symptoms during the 4-6 weeks it takes antidepressants to take effect.
- To assist with sleeping, as without enough sleep, there is less energy to manage life, deal with symptoms and make progress in treatment.
- To assist managers in having more control when fire fighters and exiles have been in control of the client's life.
- To help with other diagnosis e.g., depression, bipolar disorder, and ADHD. Some of these disorders may have their roots in a person's trauma history and clear up during the trauma treatment. Even in this case, medications can be helpful.

Medication use must be monitored. As progress is made, and the client's needs change, it should be adjusted. Eventually the client will manage on less medication and then on none unless there is an underlying reason for it. Decrease in medication use is one way of noticing progress.

Case Examples Illustrating Medication Use

Example: When Tom began treatment he was unable to control his self- destructive firefighter behaviors which included cutting and getting himself sexually abused by various men. He did not want to go on medication, and his therapist agreed, as long as he could stop his self-destructive behaviors and make progress in therapy. This he was unable to do, so he reluctantly agreed to a trial on medication. Once he began taking a combination of mood stabilizers, antidepressants, and PRN Klonopin (clonazepam), he began making progress. In the middle of his treatment, he was able to go off the psychiatric medication and continue making progress. Presently, he continues to use a small amount of medical marijuana to manage chronic physical and emotional pain.

Example: Because Tracey was at high risk of suicide, acting out violently, and needing hospitalization, she remained on atypical antipsychotic medication and PRN Ativan (lorazepam) throughout much of her treatment. Ativan was often used when trauma work was done, because some of her parts had violent and homicidal impulses which had, at times, been acted on. It provided both her and her therapist with extra control and safety. The medication was adjusted as she made progress, until she no longer needed it and done with treatment. Eventually, she realized she was struggling with a low level of constant depression and decided to go on a relatively small dose of an antidepressant. She likens her medication usage to that of a diabetic person taking insulin and continues on it to this day.

Example: Caroline used PRN Ativan when she had flashbacks around anniversary dates. She also used it for situations which she dreaded, e.g., meetings with her boss who reminded exiles of her sadistic grandmother. This minimized the amount of anxiety she felt during these meetings and enabled her to interact appropriately with her boss versus being inarticulate from terror. After the meetings, instead of feeling drained for the rest of the day, she could function. The parts felt supported by the Ativan. Additionally, this was one of the things that helped them realize that, in the present, they could get help and/or take action to help themselves, in contrast to the past when they could only endure. The comparative calmness experienced on the PRN Ativan enabled parts to be able to take in real time information about the boss, which began to lessen their automatic negative transference reactions.

Example: Leslie began treatment needing relatively high doses of psychiatric medication. As treatment progressed, she was able to go down on the doses. Subsequently, new traumatic material emerged. Leslie felt hopeless and despairing about ever being done with treatment. The therapist pointed out that they were now able to work on this more severe traumatic material because she was able to function on less medication than in earlier stages of treatment. This concrete indication of progress was helpful.

Negative Physiological Results of Not Being Medicated and/or Under Medicated

When clients have flashbacks, backlash, and/or anxiety attacks, etc., their bodies become flooded with cortisol and various neurotransmitters. When this causes self-destructive behaviors, endorphins are released. Endorphins, also released when people take opioids, add a physically addictive component to self-destructive behaviors. As neurologists note , nerves that fire together wire together (or remained wired together). These loops of symptoms maintain negative neuropathways that need to be healed. Yes, some people can endure their symptoms and heal and don't need the support of medication. For others, not being on medication can make any therapy impossible, or it can lengthen and complicate their treatment and life. In these cases, medication can be necessary to achieve positive results.

Evaluating and Working with Medication Providers

It is unfortunately not possible to blindly rely on the skill of medication providers. Like therapists, many have little or no training in working with complex trauma disorders and dissociation and are not aware of how to adequately prescribe, although some think they do. Ideally, find a medication provider who knows the range of medications that are useful for people with severe trauma disorders and who will listen to you and your client. Also:

1. Learn what medications can be helpful so you can suggest them to a medication provider who is not familiar with these medications, and who ideally, will do a little research if unfamiliar about how to use them.
2. Primary care physicians are often willing to prescribe PRN's and antidepressants, although they can be overly reliant on, and may need to be discouraged from, prescribing Xanax (Alprazolam)(more addictive) versus the less addictive Ativan (lorazepam) or Klonopin (clonazepam). Some clients who are too anxious to see a medication specialist will be willing to see their primary care physician. This can be a great first step to seeing a medication provider if a more involved medication evaluation is necessary.
3. Some medication providers can be excellent about medicating but may not know much or anything about working with dissociated parts or IFS. They may be in denial about the very existence of dissociative disorders

in spite of their being listed in the DSM since 1982. In this case, I tell clients that the therapy is done in therapy sessions, and their medication provider is just for medication. The client is responsible for checking with parts to see if they have any questions and is also responsible for making sure all questions get answered.

Working with Parts around Medication

Three clients influenced my approach to working with parts around medication. The first client was severely depressed in spite of being on a high dose of an antidepressant. Internal exploration revealed a severely depressed exile who did not know the medication was for her. Once she realized the medication was for her and she began taking it with the other parts, the depression lessened significantly, and the dosage was lowered. The second client stayed awake throughout a colonoscopy despite her doctor giving her *"enough medication to knock over a horse."* After negotiating with parts who as children had been *"given candy"* i.e., drugs and then abused, the most frightened ones agreed to stay at "my office" during medical procedures and allow whatever anaesthesia was needed to work for the two parts who attended procedures. The third example extended this approach to food, vitamins, and drinking liquids. A client was referred to me diagnosed with a "treatment resistant binge eating disorder" and an undiagnosed dissociative disorder. She reported being starved as a child, along with other abuses. The child part that held the experience and the feelings of being starved, binged whenever she got out because she was afraid she would never be fed again. She did not know food at meals was now for her too because it wasn't when she was a child. Once the adult part told her, *"All the meals, snacks, and drinks are for you too!"* and reminded her of this at every meal, the binging stopped.

Negotiating with Parts Around Taking Medication

The following sections are steps in negotiating with parts around taking medication. I began following this procedure in 2001 and have continued to refine it:

Psychoeducation Around Medication Consultations

As a client and I discuss the possibility of a medication consultation, all parts who are willing are asked about their concerns and for input. It may help to reinforce that a medication consult is just that, a consultation. After the consultation, the client has control and choices over what they do with the prescription. They can decide to fill it or wait and discuss it more in therapy. Once the prescription is filled, the client also has control over trying it or not, and how much to try. All discussions are done with as many parts as possible participating or being spoken for.

Example: A client had a history of sadistic abuse, including being drugged and raped as a very young child. She had flashbacks so intense she had to hide in a closet, cut herself around certain anniversary dates and was generally tortured by anxiety. For the first years of therapy, she also had flashbacks whenever the possibility of medication was brought up. It was necessary to avoid the mention of medication, and so I referred to it as the "*M word.*" Eventually she was able to consider the possibility of taking medication and got a prescription for low dose Ativan. It took a year for her to fill the prescription and then she carried the Ativan in her purse for another 2 years. Finally enough parts were willing to discuss a plan to try the Ativan.

As we began making the plan, I asked her to *lightly* scan through her body.

> Note: The word "lightly" is deliberately used here, to avoid the full intensity of the somatic feelings.

She noted tension and a sense of dread. She asked the parts with those feelings and concerns to relax back until she felt at least a small amount of curiosity/Self energy towards the parts. They wanted her to know they were anxious, and two parts didn't want to try it at all. They were reminded that they had choices so any parts who didn't want to try the medication didn't have to. They agreed to watch and to allow the medication to work for the other parts. We also decided that she would begin with taking just a crumb of an Ativan (less than 1/4th) with me in session.

The next session, she took the crumb, and immediately began to feel the room *"spinning around."* Because Ativan takes some minutes to take effect, it was easy to know that these symptoms were flashbacks. I said, *"It's a flashback. The medication hasn't had time to take effect. Let the parts inside and everyone else know that it's safe to try this. The doctor who prescribed it is one you've checked out for years, you're here with me, and there's no danger."* She felt a bit of relief, and then felt nauseous. With my coaching, she connected with another part having a flashback and reassured her. This continued for 20 minutes until the parts began to feel safe enough and noticed they were still fully able to walk, talk and think for themselves. We repeated this for 2 more sessions then increased the amount to two crumbs. Eventually, the client was able to choose to take the PRN at home when she was anxious.

In addition to helping her take medication, this process helped her begin to differentiate her childhood experience of being drugged and raped, from taking medication prescribed by a doctor whom she had checked out as an adult. The purpose of medication prescribed in the present was to help her have more control, more choices, and to have a way to take care of her body during difficult times. The purpose of the pills she was given as a child was to control, confuse, and quiet her while she was abused.

She felt more confident and could relax more knowing that if she needed to take an Ativan, she had them with her. She ended up taking very few and they were very helpful.

Example: A client was started on an antidepressant. After negotiating with parts, they agreed to take one. Two weeks later, they tried another one. After parts observed the result of taking the medication and were reassured that *"nothing bad was going to happen"* they began to use it as prescribed.

Because these clients tend to suffer from hopelessness, learned helplessness, and all or nothing thought patterns, it is helpful to let them know that they are (if they choose) doing a trial on medication, not signing up to take it forever. I suggest that clients consider a three-month trial, then together we evaluate how it is working. Ultimately, the client decides whether to continue it or not. Of course, the length of trial is agreed upon and can be changed at any time.

As I discuss medication with people who don't want the side effects or to *"pollute"* their body, I tell them two things, namely, that one, *"Medications have side effects, but not taking medications have side effects too. All those neurotransmitters running rampant in your body are having an impact plus symptoms, are slowing down your healing process."* And two; *"We're talking a medication trial here, not you taking it for a lifetime."*

Psychoeducation on Taking Medication

When the client gets medication and is ready to take it, I suggest that when it's taken, the client remind all parts who are willing to take it, to take it while visualizing the medication taking effect and reaching every cell of the body.

I then ask any parts who are not willing to take the medication, to watch the parts who are, and as the medication takes effect to notice how it impacts them. I then suggest, that after carefully observing, if it looks like something they would be willing to try, perhaps someday they can. These parts do not even have to let me, or the client know they have tried it, they can just take *"a sip"* of the medication and see what it's like, and then decide if they want to ever try it again.

This process has worked well with clients. There have, however, been reports of medication *"not working"* for dissociative disordered clients. In my opinion, this is often due to the nature of dissociative disorders and polarized parts who are blocking the medication effects, rather than the medications themselves.

> Note: Getting all the parts to agree to take medication is not practical, because of the many polarizations in these systems and a fundamental lack of trust. I sometimes say to clients, *"If I grew up in your family, I wouldn't trust anyone (including me) either."* Also, in complex systems, there are often dissociated layers of parts who aren't part of the initial treatment. These layers generally contain burdens of more difficult traumatic material and should not be accessed until it is the right time to work with them. Respect for parts is key and helps to differentiate the past (where there was no respect) from the present. If a part doesn't want to take medication, that choice is respected

Cuing Medication Effects: Cuing is a hypnotic technique that provides a shortcut to somatic and emotional feelings. It is also taught during EMDR training specifically to cue the feelings of being in one's safe space (see Chapter 4). Here, it is being used to cue medication effects. Like everything, cuing can be used for good or for evil. Several examples of negative cuing are described in Anna Salter's book, *Transforming Trauma* (1995) e.g., when a perpetrator appeared perfectly appropriate during a supervised visit, but had prepared himself for the visit by washing himself with the same soap he used before molesting his daughter. The fragrance of the soap had become a cue to being raped.

Suggested Psychoeducation on Cuing

"When you hammer a light switch onto a wall, you can turn it on and off, but it doesn't work until it is wired. We're going to wire or cue the feelings of taking medication, so you can either use the cue to speed up the effect of taking medication, or use your cue to enable you to somatically bring up the effect of taking medication.

We all have somatic memory. Research shows that when we think about an activity, we're familiar with, and visualize it happening, all the muscles that respond when we engage in the activity respond. This phenomenon is often used in sports performance training, e.g., basketball players who visualize shooting foul shots over and over actually improve their accuracy. You have somatic memories for bad stuff which you notice when you have flash backs. Cuing medication impact is a positive use of that ability."

Scripts used in this book are meant to be guidelines not to be used rigidly.

Installing and Practicing the Cue

Once the client describes the impact of the medication working, identify what the client wants to use as a cue. Cues can be words such as "Calm" or an image like a tight rubber band becoming loose and relaxed, or a physical cue such as putting the thumb and middle finger together. There are two possibilities for "wiring" the cue (as in the light switch metaphor). (1) It can be installed using 6 or less slow bilateral taps, as taught in EMDR training. Or the client can simply visualize and feel into the memory of the somatic feelings. Suggest that the client, *"Picture and feel the medication working, feel it going to every cell of your body."*

Bilateral tapping is preferred to EMDR eye movements as research shows that tapping is not as powerful as eye movements and works slower. With complex trauma clients, slower means more control and safety, therefore, use bilateral tapping.

> If you are new to bilateral tapping, practice it on yourself before using it with clients. Timing is roughly one tap per second. Clients can self-tap from one knee to the other, tap one foot then the next, or use the Butterfly hug (Artigas, 1998) by crossing their arms in front of their body and tapping on the upper arms.

As always when working with people with parts, it is necessary to ask all parts who are willing to participate, and help other parts learn how to use the cue.

The client's homework is to first use the cue while taking medication and noticing it taking effect. Then to practice the cue while reminding themselves of the medication's effect. Eventually, sometimes immediately, many clients can simply use the cue and feel the somatic effect of having taken medication.

Example: Tracey would sometimes take an Ativan when she got triggered. As the Ativan took effect, she noticed her shoulders would relax, her thoughts stopped racing, and she began to be able to think clearer. As her thoughts slowed down, she could remember to use her coping skills, she noticed she could breathe easier, and she felt less anxious. I asked her to recall those feelings in her body (somatic memory), we installed them, and then cued them as a short cut to the positive feelings. She practiced using her cue at home, and then, when triggered, she could use her PRN Ativan, or she could use her cue which we jokingly referred to as *"faux Ativan."*

Example: A woman was highly asthmatic, had numerous ER visits, and used 12 inhalers. I had her and the parts to focus the feeling of using the inhaler, including the blast of cold air as she used it, the taste of it, her feeling her airways and lungs opening, and the message that *"the medication is going to just where it is needed"*. The cue word was "inhaler". She was instructed to bring up the feeling of using her inhaler and her cue word 6 times a day (per usual behavioral medicine instructions). She quickly reduced her inhaler use from 12 to 2 and has not had any more ER visits in over 10 years.

Summary

This chapter discussed the uses and advantages of appropriate use of medication to reduce symptoms and assist with client stability, the disadvantages of not taking medication, and some of the complexities involved in talking to clients about medications. As dissociated parts appear to have the ability to block medication effects, the process of negotiating the taking of medication is discussed. It is not necessary for all parts to take the medication and it is important to respect the parts who initially refuse. This is clinically important, as respect was not something these clients experienced during childhood. These parts are negotiated with so they can allow others to take the medication while they watch. This process teaches and reinforces the need for negotiating and collaboration among parts.

This and other interventions are done to support progress towards integrated functioning, and the eventual goal of living a Self-led life.

CHAPTER 10

Introduction to Phase-Oriented Treatment

"The definition of Insanity is doing the same thing over and over again and expecting different results." Albert Einstein

"We know when someone says they're in IFS treatment, it means they're in trouble." Moderator of an online discussion list for people with dissociative disorders.

Phase-oriented trauma treatment, first used in the late nineteenth century by Pierre Janet, is a three-phase model that provides safety, grounding, and efficiency in healing, and integrates productively with IFS. It is the standard of care for clients with complex trauma related and dissociative disorders (D. Brown et al. 2011, Chu 2011, Courtois and Ford 2013, Herman 1997, Howell 2011, ISSTD 2011, Loewenstein and Welzant 2010, Van der Hart et al. 2006). Research shows that it decreases symptoms of people with dissociative disorders (Brand and Loewenstein 2014).

The 3 phases of phase-oriented treatment of trauma are as follows:

1. Establishing the treatment. Developing coping and stabilization skills, internal communication, cooperation, and compassion among parts. Orienting parts to the present.

2. Paced uncovering and healing of traumatic material.
3. Integration and self-development, adjusting to a life not organized around trauma

Although listed linearly, the stages are not rigid. For instance, if during Phase 2 a client is experiencing backlash or is becoming increasingly symptomatic during the week, the treatment goes back to Phase 1 to restabilize and better prepare the client for Phase 2, rather than continuing trauma work and witnessing, which runs the risk of further destabilizing the client. This circle back into Phase 1 may take a shorter or longer amount of time depending on why the client had difficulty staying stable in Phase 2. During Phase 3 an unhealed burden may surface, resulting in a return to Phase 2 or even to Phase 1.

Differentiating Phase-Oriented Treatment from IFS

Standard IFS is a powerful therapy modality and works extremely well for many people, generally those with less complex trauma disorders and with more capacity to unblend parts from Self. Perhaps this is why IFS has developed an adversarial view towards phase-oriented treatment, despite the fact that phase-oriented treatment has been used to comprehensively heal people with C-PTSD and dissociative disorders long before IFS was developed. It is helpful to know what phase-oriented treatment is and is not, and where it is similar to IFS.

Like IFS, phase-oriented treatment considers all parts as helpful, important, and as having contributed to survival. No competent therapist works on getting rid of parts, as all parts belong to the whole person. Therapists who have tried to banish parts only succeed in suppressing them, which re-enacts parents' denial of their children's needs and feelings. This results in treatment failures and delays, and ultimately complicates therapy even once the client has begun treatment with a competent therapist

IFS teaches that people have all the resources they need to heal and once in Self, the resources will emerge. Phase-oriented treatment believes that all people are born with the capacity to heal. Because IFS believes that everyone has all the resources they need, they believe that teaching coping skills is unnecessary and insults managers who have been working hard managing. Phase-oriented treatment, a trauma therapy, recognizes that in these difficult kinds of childhoods, children do not develop the abilities they would have learned in a healthier childhood. These abilities include self-soothing, managing strong feelings, and developing a foundation of belief that if something goes wrong, things will eventually get better. These children have been brought up by very dysfunctional parents, who are suffering with their own untreated PTSD/DDs, attachment and personality disorders. They learn to cope and manage, but their coping and management skills are what their dysfunctional parents have taught them through example, and/or are how children cope in reaction to abuse and neglect.

Example: A woman has horrible pain every month when she menstruates. She deals with it by hiding and refusing to tell the doctors she is seeing about yet another chronic issue. She suffers terribly and silently. Parts connect the blood and pain with rape they were not allowed to tell anyone about. They believe suffering is her lot in life, and that it is her fault and she deserves it. They believe if she sees a doctor for that part of her body, she will be raped.

Because survival and maintaining attachment is paramount, abuse (including traumatic neglect) and the resulting overwhelming feelings needs to be dissociated, as do other aspects of life. Therapists who breach dissociative lids on traumatic material without teaching coping skills to manage traumatic material and overwhelming feelings risk clients becoming more symptomatic, flooded, overwhelmed, and at worst decompensated. Other clients end up dissociating more to avoid unleashing traumatic material. These clients may be experienced in treatment as numbed out, as not making progress, or can appear to be making progress when at a deeper level, the trauma is not being healed.

Example: A teen with a comparatively short period of abuse by a non-family member went into IFS treatment. Her extremely experienced IFS therapist did standard IFS. Witnessing with no coping skills breached the lid holding back the dissociated traumatic material and totally overwhelmed the client's inadequate ability to manage. Continued IFS led to the client becoming more and more symptomatic, needing more therapist support during the week, and her functioning, which had been good, became impaired. The client was transferred to another experienced IFS therapist who continued to do standard IFS and her condition worsened to the point of her becoming dangerously unstable. This damage on top of the original trauma took years for the client and family to begin to recover from.

Example: A woman had seven years of IFS therapy which she reported had helped her. Her IFS therapist retired and referred her to a Trauma Informed IFS therapist who recognized symptoms of dissociation. A dissociated layer of parts holding burdens of trauma was found, coping skills were developed, and the client eventually healed.

Example: A client with C-PTSD spent eight years in therapy with a skilled IFS practitioner. Over this time, she made little progress, then got more and more anxious and eventually sought consultation to determine if she should continue with her IFS therapy. After the consultation, she transferred to a Trauma Informed IFS therapist, began making steady progress, and currently feels much better.

While IFS believes that clients have all the resources they need, Phase-oriented treatment recognizes that many managers, exiles, and firefighters who have been living and coping as best as they can, eventually will become exhausted and burn out. When presented with adequate psychoeducation, new coping skills are welcomed by managers who feel supported and recognized for their hard work, by exiles who have had the incredibly difficult job of holding extreme burdens to protect other parts, and by firefighters who eventually appreciate the options available to their firefighting behaviors. Coping skills taught early in treatment also provide concrete evidence of the efficacy of treatment and help develop initial trust in the therapist. Finally coping and stabilization skills help clients function better or continue functioning at their highest level possible. They decrease unhealthy dependence on the therapist, self-destructive behaviors, backlash, and ultimately make treatment more efficient and successful.

Standard IFS believes that when asked, exiles can contain their burdens during the witnessing process, so managers and other parts do not become overwhelmed. While this may work for many, in the case of those with complex trauma disorders, burdens are often extreme or volcanic. For these clients coping skills are necessary so that exiles (and other parts) do not become overwhelmed in the process of unburdening. Even if exiles want to contain burdens and believe they can, they may be dissociated from the burdens themselves or from the intensity of the burdens, and thus not have the information needed to make an accurate judgement of their capacity. Under these circumstances, confidently telling exiles they *"can"* manage burdens adds an additional layer of shame when they inevitably fail or struggle.

IFS tends to do direct access for as limited time as possible, and much of the work is done through Self to part. Phase-oriented therapy has no concept of Self or Self energy which is initially helpful with these clients as being in Self during their childhoods was dangerous and not supported. Thus, the discussion of the power of Self is contraindicated with people who have been severely punished for showing bits of Self energy. These clients often feel like their self (small "s" to distinguish it from IFS's Self) has been shattered, they may not have a concept of being or an understanding of who they are. Patiently using direct access for as long as necessary and developing Self energy among parts eventually leads to these clients being able to access Self.

Through direct access, parts are encouraged to develop system-wide communication, cooperation, and compassion for each other. In other words, parts are encouraged to develop Self energy. Parts are also taught to help each other remember coping skills, to develop teams to manage different requirements of life (see Chapter 11. Section 1) and needs. For instance, a client may have one part who takes care of a group of young exiles.

Conclusion to Phase One Introduction

Respecting the power of trauma and teaching clients enhanced ways of coping with traumatic material supports parts by giving them more control and more choices. Phase-oriented treatment believes in supporting clients in maintaining their highest level of functioning. Symptoms and distress during the week are managed with coping skills. Phase 1 development of coping and stabilization skills assists with Phase 2 paced uncovering of traumatic material. Phase 3 deals with whatever the client needs to adjust to living a life not organized around trauma.

When preparing for sessions it is always important for the therapist to be in Self. With this population, this is especially important as some communication will always be nonverbal (see Chapter 3). When the therapist is in Self there is an energetic pull for the Self of the client, Self of the parts and Self energy in general. Additionally, I surround the client with an energy field of soft confidence that healing is possible.

Note: Expressing too much confidence and hope often creates backlash in these clients who are for the most part, filled with hopelessness and shame. Express all feelings in a moderate way and watch how the client responds. It is also important to realize that the part who is present may be responding very differently than other parts inside.

A useful review of treating clients with DID is available online: Guidelines for treating dissociative identity disorder in adults, third revision. *Journal of Trauma & Dissociation*, (2011) 12(2): 115–187. (Chu, J. A., et al.)

CHAPTER 11

Phase One: Establishing the Treatment, Developing Coping and Stabilization Skills

After an overview of Phase One and Phase One tasks, this chapter includes sections which elaborate on three of the tasks: Daily Life Teams, Daily Morning Homework, and Orienting Parts to the Present, also Known as Retrieval.

The following list of Phase 1 tasks is not linear and are accomplished via clinical judgement and client necessity. Many are woven into early sessions as questions and issues lead towards them. There are clients who accomplish this phase quickly and others who need more time, especially if they are coming to you from inadequate therapy experiences. With some clients, I have done safe space imagery in the first session and begun working on communication among parts. With others e.g., a 78-year-old with a fifty-year history of therapy (including several years of IFS) where dissociative barriers were breached and exiles and managers became totally overwhelmed, there was initially chaos.

Phase One Tasks

- Establish the treatment relationship.
- Create an atmosphere of relative safety and trust.

- Establish boundaries.
- Clarify diagnosis and/or discern how dissociated parts are from each other (see Chapter 5).
- Introduce the topic of parts carefully. If this is too destabilizing, wait until it isn't.
- Get to know the available layer of parts: who are there, what is their function, and how they help the system. Do not seek out every part in the system as it can complicate the treatment. Instead allow deeper layers of parts to remain dissociated until initial trauma work is done, and they naturally surface.
- Help the client maintain and upgrade their dissociative defenses.
- Develop internal communication and cooperation among parts who are present.
- Daily Morning Homework (Section 1).
- Develop coping skills for all available parts (see Chapter 4).
- Develop daily life teams (Section 2). Work on orienting parts to the present, more expanded steps toward retrieval (Section 3).
- Provide knowledge on neurology.
- Assess the need for a medication consultation (see Chapter 9).

Establishing the Treatment Relationship

The goal in establishing the treatment relationship is to create a collaborative relationship with enough trust and safety that the client can be in therapy with you. In the first session, I let the client know it's okay to:

- Ask any questions they all have.
- To not answer questions if they do not want to.

- Tell me if I got something wrong and if something feels wrong or is missing in the therapy.
- Let me know if they need something,
- Tell me if I forgot something e.g., if I said I'd call you and forget.

Because these clients grew up in families where their needs were not recognized, allowed, or when allowed were used against them, they tend to be unassertive, suffer from learned helplessness, and have difficulty expressing their thoughts and feelings. They may have been punished for disagreeing with parents and thus fear correcting any mistakes you make. All of this is helped by the therapist modelling positive relationship behavior, e.g., by being open, listening, encouraging, and by respecting the client's input. It is also important for therapists to recognize mistakes and apologize, as in, "*I was thinking about our meeting last week* (thinking about the client during the week and telling them supports good attachment) *and realized that I forgot to tell you I can't meet next week at our usual time because I have a dentist appointment. Sorry about that. Can we reschedule?*" or "*I was thinking about you-all last week and realized that I think we need to work more with that group of exiles. What do you-all think of that?*" The therapist taking responsibility for mistakes and allowing choices will need to be repeatedly demonstrated to guard against automatic compliance and inability to express needs.

Create an Atmosphere of Relative Safety and Trust

Developing safety and trust is often mentioned as a prerequisite for therapy however many of these clients are rightfully mistrustful of the expectation of any trust or safety. A good place to start developing a foundation for trust is to appreciate this simple fact which I sometimes verbalize as, "*If I grew up in your family,*

I wouldn't trust anyone either." Acknowledging this reality begins to lay the basis for clients learning how to trust and begins the therapeutic relationship on a foundation of understanding with reasonable expectations.

Using the words "*I understand*" or "*I get it*" also can create a rift when used casually without basis. It is not possible to understand what it is like to grow up in a very complicated family. Seeking to understand and being curious is more helpful.

Example: A client once asked, *"Do you understand how depressed I am?"* I answered, *"I remember what it was like when I was the most depressed in my life, multiply it several times, and then I think I get close to understanding how depressed you are."*

The question *"Do you understand?"* in this case was a wish on some level and a test on another. Sitting in the office with a client does not automatically give anyone an understanding of the desolation and depression experienced by those who were severely neglected and abused by family members who should have been protecting and caring for their children. That you strive to understand (verses automatic, assumptive understanding) is another building block for developing a respectful treatment relationship.

Example: A client got upset and slammed the door on their way out of a session. This was a bold positive move for this client who had been trapped literally and figuratively during their childhood. Eventually the client was able to leave sessions and come back after a few minutes, and then to progress to using words to discuss distress.

Establish Boundaries

As with beginning any therapeutic relationship, an initial task is to establish the treatment frame, and boundaries. This is particularly important, as Kluft (1993) noted, DID "*is a condition created by broken boundaries…Therefore, a successful treatment will have a secure treatment frame and consistent boundaries..."* The concrete details in setting the treatment frame include discussing basic expectations re payment, the policy on session scheduling, cancelation, and in between session contact.

This may be covered in initial paperwork and needs to be gone over verbally. Boundaries will be tested and/or broken in the process of clients learning to have good boundaries and healing. This provides an opportunity to rework and establish healthy boundaries

> Note: In between session contact can be an area of difficulty for many therapists new to working with people with complex trauma histories. Out of caring, therapists can become too responsive to desperate clients and encourage in between session calls, texts, and e-mails. It can feel like the right thing to do, it can feel helpful (and sometimes is), and then it can become excessive as some clients become overly dependent on the therapist grounding them versus learning and using coping skills. It is imperative for therapists and clients to focus on learning and using coping skills.

Clarify Diagnosis and/or How Dissociated Parts Are:

As mentioned in Chapter 5, diagnosis can be simple if the client has the answers to questions about dissociative symptoms and phenomena, or more complicated if the answers are dissociated or the client needs to hide it. Diagnostic questions need to be added to all initial sessions to screen for the possibility of a dissociative disorder.

Why It is Important to be Careful When Introducing Parts

Think about a child who is raped at night, then has to get up the next morning and eat breakfast with the rapist and other family members all of whom are acting like nothing happened. Then she goes to school to learn and socialize. The child cannot deal with these conflicting realities and eventually, one part handles the nightly rapes, another handles breakfast and after school interactions with her family, and another part handles school and friends. The part who carries attachment to her parents does not know about the rapes at night. The part who handles the rapes believes she is bad and that is why they keep happening. The part who handles school does not know about the rapes because she handles interactions outside of the home and might make the mistake of telling someone, which she has been told would result in the death of everyone she loves. In addition, the part who goes to school has to be able to learn and to be able to do that the rapes need to be dissociated. The parts have to be secret from each other and have to keep secrets from external people. The girl needs to keep looking like she's "fine" or the secret will be found out, and she will be beaten or die. She survives by parts not knowing about each other and by no one knowing about the parts. This way she manages an extremely confusing traumatic childhood, and comes out of it with an education, a job, the possibility of a life and a dissociative disorder. One theory is that people who are born without the talent to dissociate do not make it out of these childhoods with enough capacity to heal.

As disconnection/dissociation and secrecy meant survival, a therapist who starts talking about parts may be perceived of as dangerous. It is important to watch for dissociative symptoms, evaluate how comfortable the client is as you begin introducing the language of IFS, and to slow down the process if the client's distress level increases. Normalize the presence of parts, but do not be overly curious or enthusiastic about them or IFS. Watch carefully for the client's response. If the client looks blank, hesitant, gets quiet or anxious, slow down. You may want to ask your client, "*What's it like for you to think about working with parts?*" Also, pay attention to your countertransference feelings as you ask questions. If you feel like you are not connecting with the client, feel a sense of emptiness or distress, you may be picking up on nonverbal communication from the client. Giving diagnostic tests like the Dissociative Experience Scale can help (or asking questions from the DES and/or other diagnostic tests), because it shows the client that you know something about dissociation and gives them words to describe symptoms. Some clients will be dissociated from parts and have no conscious awareness of them.

With clients who are uneasy with a mention of parts it can be helpful to ease into the discussion *by* identifying parts, as in this example*: "There's the side of you who knows you are competent and there is a side of you who thinks you aren't."* Or: "*You know you are competent and can teach really well, but in front of an audience 'another you' kind of loses that knowledge and gets anxious.*"

It is often helpful and normalizing to mention your own parts. I begin doing this in an offhand way. I might say:" *It's so beautiful out today and I really wanted to garden, but the practical me said, it's too hot! Work now, garden later!*" Or:" *One part of me wanted to get up this morning, and another wanted to stay in bed and read.*"

While there are clients who are afraid of anyone knowing they have parts, there are also clients who are happy and relieved to hear that you are a therapist who knows people have parts. One client said, "*You know about parts, do other people? I thought I was crazy.*" Others have concerns that can be easily addressed, e.g., "*I hear voices in my head, am I psychotic?*"

Example: A "really nice woman" (quote from the referring therapist) came in describing symptoms of anxiety, feeling depressed, disconnected, and having difficulty making friends. After hearing a little about the woman's struggles, the therapist began talking about parts following the IFS recommendation to: "*Attach the word 'part' to each of (the client's) struggles ... introducing the idea that they have different parts.*" (Anderson, p. 25, 2021) The client acted interested, made a second appointment, but never came back, and refused all contact with the therapist.

Some months later, the client coincidently came into treatment with me. After I provided psychoeducation on having parts, talked about my own parts, and discussed safety considerations, e.g., "*Our sessions are totally private. No one is allowed to know anything about you unless you give me specific permission.*" she was able to slowly begin acknowledging her parts. At one point she said, "*It terrifies me when you talk about parts. You're not supposed to know about them.*"

Example: A man waited for months for an opening because he had DID. When he began treatment, he said he did not have DID or parts. It took time for him to feel comfortable acknowledging parts and to work openly with them.

Example: A client tested low on the Dissociative Experience Scale (DES). Three months later, the client began talking about losing time and being confused by finding a kind of cereal he'd never eaten in his cupboard. Later it became clear that the client did not initially feel comfortable answering questions from the DES. Once he knew the therapist better, he began talking about dissociative symptoms using language from the DES.

Example: A woman became extremely distressed whenever parts were mentioned. Eventually, we were able to refer to them as the "P Word." Eventually, she could tolerate me referring to them as "the parts you don't have." Then we were able to work with them.

Psychoeducation on Having Parts and Getting to Know Them

Clients often need psychoeducation about why it is okay to have parts, and why it is safe to talk about them now. I sometimes start with: *"Many people have a sense of an inner child who holds some of the misery from their childhood, I'm wondering if you have a sense of a child part of you like that."*

If the client denies having parts, but seems open to hearing why I'm asking, I might say, *"We all have parts."* And I give them my version of Ego State 101, as follows:

Ego State 101: *"We all have parts. There's the part of me that wanted to lie in bed this morning, eat bon bons, and read, and another part of me that said, 'Get up! You like working!' There's the kid part of me that plays with the neighbour kids, the couch potato me that sometimes watches too much TV, the relaxed professional me like I am now, and the hyper professional me when I give talks or testify in court. For me, there's a free flow of information among the parts of me, and if I need to switch from one to another, like if I'm playing with a kid friend and suddenly there is an emergency, I can switch smoothly to adult mode. If you have had a complicated childhood, it can be like there are cement walls among the parts. You can get stuck in one part and not have access to the others, and not have a free flow of information. So you might get stuck in a child part of you and not have access to information older parts have."*

This is normalizing as is the IFS message that we all have parts.

Once parts can be discussed with the client, it is important to perform the following actions:

1. Identify and connect with the more accessible parts of the mind (either separately, or through the adult/manager/Self-like part).

Phase One: Establishing the Treatment, Developing Coping and Stabilization Skills

2. Begin to develop internal communication and cooperation among parts (Kluft, 1999).
3. Use "talking through." This is a standard therapeutic technique for those with dissociated parts. Simply the therapist refers to *"you-all"* or says *"I want everyone to listen."* This is efficient and helps lead to integrative functioning.

Some people with DID/OSDD have complex systems with many layers of parts. Do not activate parts in different layers as that makes the work overly complicated and adds to the possibility of overwhelm. Some therapists believe that all parts should be included in all of the treatment. This is not practical or helpful for those with many parts.

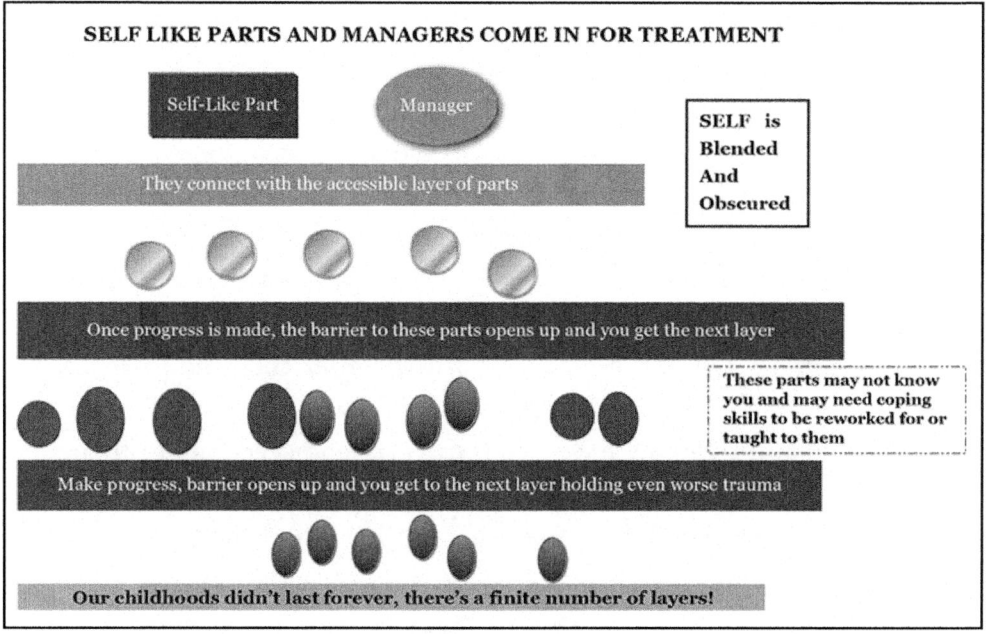

Example: One client worked with a therapist who encouraged him to meet all of his parts. He eventually connected with over 80 parts. This slowed down his healing as it was impossible to work with all the parts at once and since they had been activated, they all wanted attention.

Key Strategies for Getting to Know Parts

Different clients have different responses to finding out that they have parts and/or that to heal, they need to get to know them. Some have actively suppressed parts either unconsciously or consciously and have been running their lives without any knowledge or real connection to their systems. For them, it is a shock to find out that to heal, they need to accept, get to know, and work with all the parts in their system.

One woman said, *"I hate those whiny parts of me. They've been ruining my life for years."* To clients like her I say, *"It makes sense that you aren't interested in knowing yourself as a whole person. Your parents weren't interested in you as a whole person. They wanted you to be compliant, to not complain, to not ask for help, etc. But we need to do better than your parents."* I might also say, *"You've been trying to get rid of the parts for years and it hasn't worked. Let's try it my way."* Or, *"If we could work on you healing without you working with parts, I would do it. But that would be a waste of time and I'm not doing anything that slows down your healing."* I say these things along with compassion and acceptance of their grief and loss. Imagine what it would be like to suddenly find out that you are one of many and that you suddenly have to get to know and accept all of them to heal.

Others will have more awareness of parts and have an easier time connecting with many of the parts in their systems.

There are several ways to assist with parts getting to know each other. IFS language can be extremely helpful. For instance, I might say: *"Focus lightly* (note: "lightly" as in this population feelings can be extremely strong) *on the anxiety. Where do you feel it in and around your body?... Ask the part holding this feeling (these feeling, this belief, the image etc.) to give you some space or sit next to you. We don't want the part to go away, this will help us get to know the part."* Or *"Focus lightly on the anxiety and notice how you're feeling toward the part who's holding it."* If the manager/adult/ or other part (at times systems are entirely run by child parts) says, *"I hate that part."* I explain, *"There's no way we're going to get to know that part if you're feeling hatred towards it. Ask the hatred to relax back for a few minutes, see if that's ok."* It is important to ask about concerns, and to ask the part to hold on to traumatic material and feelings so as to not flood the system. Much of connecting with parts or the lack thereof comes from the amount of willingness of the manager/adult.

Look for and work with very tiny bits of Self energy.

Example: Sasha was aware of a part who was angry.

I asked, *"Can you feel a little bit of interest towards this part?"*

Sasha said, *"No, I'm not interested in that part. It's too angry."*

I said, *"OK, so let the part know that you notice the part. And let the part know you're not ready to get to know it, is that all right?"* ("noticing" is a bit of Self energy)

"Yes."

"Honesty is important and you can't lie inside! So let the part know you aren't ready to get to know it, but you're working with me and you want to heal. And that I'm saying, 'To heal you need to get to know the parts and understand them. So, eventually you will, but not now...' And I want the part to know (here I directly address the part), *I know you are there and won't forget. If it seems like we are forgetting about you, you can always let me know."* (Note: Here I am giving some power to the part.) One client translated my instructions into, *"That bitch Joanne says I have to get to know you. I don't want to but I'm working with her, so I guess at some point I'll be stuck doing it."*

Note: There are important messages in this exchange. Interest is a less intense form of curiosity. It and noticing are whiffs of Self energy. Many abusive parents do not notice their children especially if they are having feelings and needs that are not approved of or the parents are dissociated themselves. The client being honest with parts is supported. And the part gets the message that although the adult (or what passes for the adult) is not ready to get to know it yet, it will happen.

As parts learn to tolerate and work with tiny bits of Self energy, the capacity of parts to allow Self energy grows. Noticing leads to interest which leads to curiosity, which is easier than compassion. Curiosity about a part does not mean a part is cared for or liked but allows an opening for communication and learning about each other. Increasing the capacity for Self energy comes with the client realizing that the present is different from the past. Now Self energy isn't punished.

> Note: One hallmark of Self-like parts are those who say early on, "*I have compassion for all my parts.*" Or "*I love all my parts.*"

On the way to parts becoming able to access Self energy when parts, I may say something half in jest and half in earnest like, "*Come on, drum up some curiosity for this kid part or she's never going to talk to you. Think about an owner of a dog screaming at it to 'come', and the dog's like: 'No Way'!! Tap into a little curiosity about who this part is and why is she the way she is. I want you all to heal and I don't want it to take forever!*" I think of this as Combat IFS!

Other possibilities include having the client keep a journal that is for all parts to write in. I suggest having a set time, like at 7:30 PM to write for fifteen minutes to one half hour. Or just for 5 minutes or 2 minutes. Having choices and control is an important part of healing.

Giving homework is always interesting. Sometimes it works the way I expect it will, and sometimes it doesn't. All results are helpful to the treatment because finding out why the homework did not work can tell you how to phrase the next set of homework or it may simply reveal useful information.

Example: A woman worked on journaling solidly for two weeks with no results. It turned out that she was sitting down and saying, "*Okay, it's time to write NOW!*" in a drill sergeant way. We laughed when we figured this out.

Example: A client stared at the journal and lost time during which no writing was done. This helped us figure out that a group of parts was blocking other parts who wanted to communicate. These blocking parts were living in the past and still believed the old message that they would be beaten for communicating anything to anyone.

Another possibility is having a client map their internal systems. One way to do this is to give the client a piece of paper. The client draws a circle where they feel they are on the map, then allows the unconscious and/or parts draw themselves wherever it feels right for them. A version of this I particularly liked was a client who made a map with post its for every part. As things were worked through and internal alliances changed, the positions of parts were easy to change.

Permission to Dissociate Traumatic Material

During this phase of treatment, clients are encouraged and given permission to continue dissociating any and/or all traumatic material related to the past. Obtaining a full history is not recommended as it can be too triggering and/or may not be possible due to how much of it has been dissociated. One metaphor for this is a Dutch door with the top half open to the present and the bottom half closed to the traumatic material. Some clients want to tell you their full history or think it is necessary. This needs to be discouraged, as it is often too triggering.

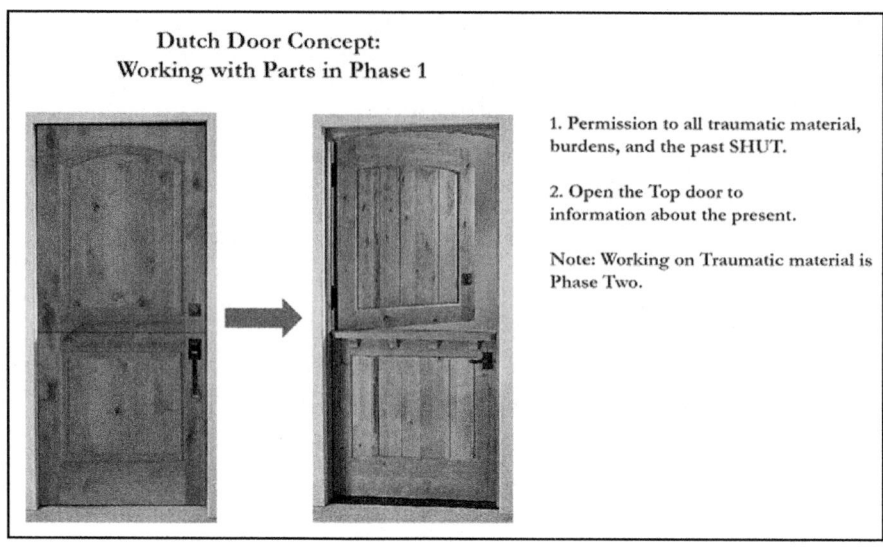

Dutch Door Concept: Working with Parts in Phase 1

1. Permission to all traumatic material, burdens, and the past SHUT.

2. Open the Top door to information about the present.

Note: Working on Traumatic material is Phase Two.

Example: A client began giving me a detailed history during her first session. I stopped and asked her what it would be like if she continued to tell me everything. She said, *"I'd end up in bed for three days."* I said, *"How about if you just give me the headlines."* The session continued and she was able to go to work after it.

Building Cooperation Among Parts

Parts in these complex systems have much to offer each other and this cooperation needs to be fostered because without cooperation among parts, progress is slower and life less manageable. As therapists, we need to notice where this is already happening, e.g., a client who drives without having accidents has parts who drive and parts who do not. An example is a client who was horrified to find out a part had gone for a 200 mile drive the night before. After checking with him to see if the car had dents or speeding tickets, I said, *"So the part who drove, is a good driver."* And the client noted, the part had also filled up the tank. I then said, *"So you don't have communication with this part yet, but the part is driving responsibly, that's great!"*

There are numerous ways of developing and fostering internal cooperation among parts. Some examples include:

- Having parts coach each other on developing Safe Spaces, Containers, and remind each other to use them when they are distressed.
- Parts noticing and helping each other with cognitive distortions. For instance, when a part is panicked, asking *"What's the evidence there's danger? What are you noticing?"*
- Coaching on orienting to the present.
- Setting up systems of caretaking e.g., an older part taking care of younger parts.
- Using parts to help with communication e.g., *"Who is close enough to the baby part to help me understand what the baby's worried about?"* Or *"Who can interpret so I can understand what the deaf parts are saying?"* (One client had a group of "deaf" parts who used sign language.)
- Parts thinking of fun things to do.
- For clients with DID, developing systems of parts taking over for each other when the part or parts who have been out are tired or triggered. In one system, the agreement became that as soon as the part who handled work got home, a part that managed home life would come out.

> Note: Child parts often have or develop capacities that are beyond their "age." It is important to not fall into the trap of thinking that they are like external children. Some parts have also been present for periods of time, for instance a part who said she was 6 to 20 years old.

The Daily Morning Homework

Daily Morning Homework (See Chapter 1, Section 1 for more details) is one exercise I recommend clients do every day as it supports orienting parts to the present and helps develop communication paths among parts. It also decreases anxiety by giving parts notice about their daily schedule. The instruction is simply: *"When you wake up in the morning, ask everyone to listen and say something like, 'This is our schedule for the day. We're going to have breakfast, then go to work from 9-3, come home, meet with Joanne on Zoom, do a little food shopping, have dinner, watch TV and then go to bed. Does anyone have any questions, concerns, or comments?"* This is to be done whether there is a response or not because as parts are being spoken to and they are responding (this is a positive suggestion) communication paths are developing. One woman spent nine months doing this exercise with no response from parts. At the same time, communications from the parts indicated that they appreciated the information and it helped. After nine months, they began responding directly to her.

Develop Coping Skills for All Available Parts

Besides information on developing skills taught in Chapter 4, people with DID benefit from being encouraged/taught to use their parts to manage life. For example, the part/s who manage work may come home tired. They can rest in their safe spaces while other parts take over to make dinner. Or, if a part is triggered, another part can take over to help. Clients can also be encouraged to have more than one part out at once/be coconscious, which for example, simplifies discussing plans. Parts working together inside, leads to more integrated functioning.

Develop Daily Life Teams (Section 2)
Orient/Retrieve Parts to the Present (Section 3)

Simple Neurology

I do not spend a lot of time talking about neurology, but it can help clients to get a quick understanding of the things they have experienced. My highly simplified explanation is:

"The left brain is where thinking, and logic happens, and non-traumatic and healed traumatic memories get stored. The speech center of the brain is also located on the left side. All of our experiences go through the primitive part of the brain (the right brain). If something is traumatic it gets stuck there. If It's not traumatic it goes over to the left side. One example of how this works is a study done in Boston on the efficiency of Prozac versus EMDR for people with PTSD (2007). They had the participants tell the story of what happened to them as if it was happening in the moment to trigger them, and then did a brain scan. The results showed that the left brain was offline, while the right brain was very activated. Then they did some EMDR sessions and, following the same procedure, did brain scans again and got very different results—now the left brain was functioning and the right brain quiet. The implication is that talk therapy (left brain) is not so useful for trauma work because when trauma (right brain) is activated the speech center of the brain is largely offline. To work on trauma, you have to use therapy that accesses the right brain like EMDR, hypnosis, ego state work, or IFS. You know how sometimes when you're talking about something that happened to you, how you can't talk about it smoothly, and stumble around? That's because of the speech center of the brain being at least partly offline."

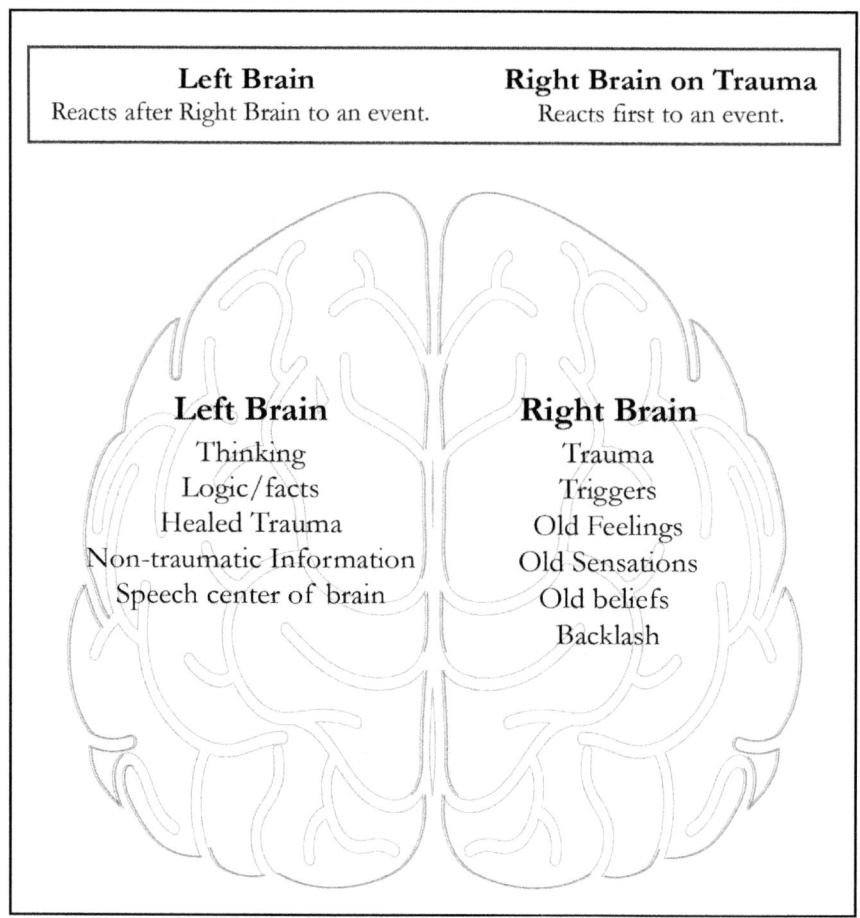

Example: One woman came in to see me and said, "*I have a great life, a great boyfriend, a terrific job, friends, and a cat. And I'm afraid all the time, I must be crazy.*" I said, "You're not crazy, it's neurology. That you have a great life, boyfriend etc. is all left-brain knowledge. Trauma gets stored in the right brain and that's not connected to the left brain. So, your left brain has the information about your current life while your right brain says: "Danger, Danger, Danger!" and is stuck in the past.

Example: A client told her talk therapist of 35 years, "*You are a terrific therapist but even a terrific therapist has to have one failure,* *and I'm your failure."* She had undiagnosed DID and a trauma history that looked like it had never been worked on.

There's a big difference between talk therapy and trauma therapy. There is also a big difference between trauma therapists who know how to work with dissociation, and those who do not.

Another helpful bit of neurology is that the right brain reacts faster than the left brain. This explains why a person can get triggered (right brain) before they remember they are safe now (left brain); also why someone automatically has a cognitive distortion before they can correct it. These explanations help decrease shame over past treatment failures and being "too crazy" to realize how great their current life is.

> Note: The terms Right and Left brains are used in the colloquial sense and are not totally accurate.

Medication

Do not discount the use of medication for this population. For some it makes treatment possible and makes their lives manageable (See Chapter 9).

The Relational Bridge

Elizabeth Howell (2011) eloquently wrote, *"The threat of 'unthinkable' agonies and the terror of going mad activate the* (internal) *self-care system, which not only restores missing aspects of the needed attachment relationships as aspects of the self but also uses such quasi-delusional methods as perceptually 'blanking out' threatening figures. The self-care system generates a sense of psychic stability by creating the illusion of sources of protection and comfort."* In highly dissociated people this self-care system is *"partially closed"*. Thus, therapists must operate as a *"relational bridge"* (Bromberg, 1998) to help clients begin to interact with the world once they are old enough to not be totally dependent on their family. Softening and evolving out of these rigid partially closed systems is helped by questions that encourage parts to think rather than continue to repeat the patterns of the past. One client eloquently described that she had lived on a *"bridge"* her whole life which really was a *"pier"* that she was unknowingly stuck on. She is now working on allowing a real bridge to relationships and life experiences.

The following is a list of helpful questions for therapists to ask clients and for clients to ask within their system of parts:

- Ask inside, who can help us understand?
- What would happen if you answered that question?
- What % of that feeling belongs to the past?
- Where does the part live (describe in picture or words)? (An orienting question)
- Who can help us understand...?
- What's the evidence?
- If you answered that question, what do you think would happen?
- How are you going to cope with impulses?
- How is that (behavior) helpful?
- What am I doing or saying that is making you anxious right now?

Example: This is an example of using some of the above with a 35-year-old woman with DID who had asked me what it was to be on a treadmill. Her experience was that once her heartbeat went up and she started breathing more rapidly, she got panicked.

I concretely described my own feelings of being on a treadmill: *"I begin walking fast, and after a few minutes, I notice that my breathing gets faster, and my heart rate goes up. This is normal."*

The client felt *"silly"* asking and was assured that she could ask me anything. I told her, it made sense that in her complicated childhood, she did not learn much about how bodies normally functioned. This normalized her lack of knowledge and decreased her shame.

Following this exchange, I asked, *"I'm curious who inside gets anxious."* (Internal communication, cooperation, compassion) (Therapist in Self modelling curiosity)

Client: *"There's a pain in the ass part who gets anxious all the time. Whenever I start breathing fast, she panics. She's a wimp."*

I noted she was blended with a critical part, asked the critical part if she could relax back and watch, and reminded the client to drum up some interest in the anxious part. Note: the client could not access Self completely, but the manager part who was present could often feel a bit of Self energy. I, *"Let the part know that you recognize that the part is there... and that you feel some interest in knowing her... Ask the part to not overwhelm you with feelings so you can start to get to know her... Is that okay with her?"*

I asked: *"What's it like for her to feel you recognize she's there.?"* The part felt uneasy that she was being noticed. I asked the client to ask the part to look through her eyes and see that she was in my office, to tell the part how long she's known me, and that no one gets hurt in my office. The client noticed the part relaxed a bit. (Note: when working with a part who has not been present, or who may not be oriented to the present, or who is probably holding burdens of old feelings, it often helps to do some simple orienting.)

The part was able to tell the client that when her heartbeat fast it meant something bad was happening.

The client was told to show the part the scene at the gym, with her gym clothes on, walking fast on the treadmill. The part was confused.

I asked her to, "*Check and see if she's still living in the past with your family.*" The part was. We agreed it made sense that the part would be afraid all the time. I then said, "*Ask her to look in your eyes—and any other parts who want to too—and as you look in her eyes, tell her that you have resources and strengths now that you did not have back then when you were her age. Show her where you live, how long you've lived there, and that you drive a car. Now let her know she can come live with you.*" (*Note: Always go for the option of more healing, if possible, especially in complicated systems of parts.)

The client said, "*She's not sure she wants to, but she says she might watch me.*" I said, "*Great, let her know she gets to decide when she wants to come into the present* (note the positive suggestion of 'when' not 'if'), *as she gets choices now* ('now' is an orienting comment). *Ask her what she wants from you in between now and next week when we meet again. She might not know, and that's OK!* (Here I am acknowledging that the part was not allowed to ask for anything in her childhood. We did not want to put pressure on the child part.) *What do you think about checking in with her during the week?*"

Client: "*I can do that if I remember.*"

Therapist: "*What does the little girl think about that?*"

"*She's not sure*"

Therapist, "*Check and see if she's ok with you checking with her if you remember, and let her know if she has a question, she can ask you. And tell her, if she wants to, she can watch you here and there, or check through your eyes and see what life today is like. She can decide.*" (Note: the part having choices and those choices being respected is a big difference from their childhood.)

A few weeks later, the client was able to ask what it felt like for the me to throw up. The client could not remember ever throwing up. Normal was not something that was allowed during her childhood, and the idea of throwing up terrified her. (We celebrated when the client threw up for the first time!)

A few weeks later, the client was able to ask what it felt in my body when I menstruated. Parts had always had flashbacks during their period as vaginal bleeding triggered having bled after being violently sexually abused.

This is an example of an exchange with a client whose physical body, physical needs, and responses were messed with, distorted, and shamed. The client felt shame asking these questions, and I said, *"Normally kids get this information from their parents. You didn't, and I'm a good person to ask. You're doing great asking these questions."*

Section 1.
Daily Morning Homework

"Daily Morning Homework" is homework that I give to all my DID and OSDD clients and to others when it is helpful. It is designed to help orient parts to their agenda for the day and make their day go smoother. It helps build trust among the system as the parts will see that what they are told, actually happens.

I explain this process by telling clients that *"Every morning when you wake up, first make sure that you are open to talking with the parts. Do this by checking in on how you feel toward parts* (a modified fire drill (see Chapter 3) process*). If you notice critical feelings, ask the part or parts holding them to relax back and let you talk with the parts. Focus in on the parts, acknowledge that they are there and ask them to listen and be open to what you are telling them. Then let them know what the agenda is for the day. When you are done, ask the parts if they have any questions, concerns, or anything to add."* Even if the client has little to no connection to the parts they still do the same homework. The client is building communication paths among the parts when parts are addressed and assisting with orienting to the present.

Benefits of Daily Morning Homework

- It helps orient parts by making them aware of what the schedule is for the present day. Parts who are not fully oriented to the present, are dissociated and/or are not connected enough, need reminders.
- This process helps build relationships among the parts because as the parts notice that what they were told actually happens they begin to learn that the adult (or whatever parts are telling them the agenda) is trustworthy.
- It decreases anxiety about events during the day, e.g., Parts will often feel anxious when there's an appointment. With this homework, they know about it in advance which helps decrease anxiety and provides a chance to decide how the appointment will be handled.
- It begins to build and develop communication paths among all the parts. Even if parts have no internal communication, addressing them and asking for input indicates that direct communication is going to happen.
- Finally, it gives the parts a chance to ask questions, add requests, and discuss concerns.

> **Note:** the qualities of Self are used and encouraged without specifically mentioning Self. This can be adjusted to more directly using qualities of Self if and when the client and parts have the capacity.

Say, *"Okay, I want everyone to listen. This is the agenda for today. We're going to get up, we're going to have breakfast, we're going to go to work from 8 to 2 and then we're going to see Joanne at 3: PM. Then we're going to go exercise. Then we're coming home and watching TV. Does anybody have any questions, concerns, or things to add?"*

Some people do this for months before they get any acknowledgement. Other people hear parts respond sooner or are already more in touch with parts. People who do not get answers may not be openly asking and may not want to connect with parts. In this case, their concerns need to be discussed. As these concerns are being worked through, I continue to support the client in completing the homework and typically suggest they say something honest like, *"I'm not interested in connecting with you, but Joanne says to heal I have to and I'm working with Joanne so I will, but I'm not ready now. But listen anyway, this is our agenda for the day."*

Client Examples of Daily Morning Homework

The following examples illustrate how parts negotiate with each other as a result of using the Daily Morning Homework.

Example: John's agenda one day went like this, *"I want everyone to listen. Today we're going to work till 2 pm and then we have our yearly doctor's appointment. Then we'll come home, eat dinner, do some emails, then watch TV. Does anyone have any concerns, questions, or comments?"* A part answered, *"I'm not going to the doctor's appointment."* This gave John and the part a chance to discuss their specific concerns about the doctor's appointment. In this case, the part was afraid the doctor would hurt them and the appointment would last for hours. John was able to reassure the part, clarify how long the appointment would last, and to suggest the part go to his safe space during the appointment and let John handle the appointment. Had John not done the morning agenda, the part would not have known about the doctor's appointment and would have been triggered. After the appointment John said he would check in with this part and let him know how the appointment went.

Example: Mary's parents were in town and planned to visit her. The morning agenda reminded parts of this. *"Today we're going to* *get up, go to group, come home and cook dinner for our parents who are coming over at 5:30. They will be going home between 8:30-9pm and will not be staying with us. I'd like anyone who doesn't want to be present to stay in their safe spaces and keep the sound- and feeling-proofing up. This will help me manage this visit. No one is allowed to hurt anyone, they will not be allowed to stay over and we will lock the house up after they leave. Any questions, concerns, or things to add?"* One child part was worried they would refuse to leave, hide in the house, and abuse her later. The adult said, *"We've done this before, and they've left every time. Sam (a friend) is going to call us at 9 PM and make sure they're gone. If they are still here, he will come right over to help."*

Example: Sage's agenda was a typical one. After going through it, one child part asked if they could buy stuffed animals, while another didn't want to go to work and wanted to play all day. Sage pointed out that they already had lots of stuffed animals, agreed to take them out after work and play with them. She then explained that the work team had to go to work because money they earned paid rent on their home, bought food, things the child parts liked like stuffed animals, and meant that they could save up to go on vacation. She suggested that the child part stay home with others and play while the work team went to work. After work they would all play with their stuffed animals, take Scooty (their dog) for a walk, then snuggle with her and watch TV. The child parts agreed to these negotiations .

Section 2. Daily Life Teams

Introduction

Parts working together is not a consciously intuitive process for dissociative clients, although much of the time unconscious teamwork is already happening. For example, many people have

Phase One: Establishing the Treatment, Developing Coping and Stabilization Skills

good driving records. That means that there is a good driver part who drives (or driver parts) and other parts who don't. If a client counters with, *"But there was the time a child part drove and we got into an accident."* I would say, *"So most of the time..."*

As in the example above, when introducing teamwork (or anything!), it's best to find evidence and talk with the client about how they already are using, in this instance, teamwork.

The steps to teamwork are:

1. Identify a need for a team.
2. Ask inside: "*Who needs to be part of this team.*"
3. Discuss it with parts.
4. Suggest the client and parts try it out and make changes if necessary.
5. Try it out for a week, and review, adjust and readjust as needed.

Example: After decompensating in therapy, losing her high-powered job, experiencing several hospitalizations and shock treatment prescribed by a "trauma" psychiatrist who had missed obvious signs of dissociation, Dora got a new therapist. With her new therapist she was diagnosed with DID and began the work of healing from her childhood and inadequate treatment. She spent time in day treatment, progressed to a job stacking shelves, and then got a new high-powered job. In preparation for beginning the new job the therapist helped Dora develop a work team made up of parts who had the necessary work skills. Other parts agreed to help by staying at home and /or in safe spaces during work time. Dora agreed to check in with them at lunch and during break times. The first 2 weeks went fine until Dora realized she was avoiding socializing and was worried co-workers would think she was stuck up. The therapist said: *"Ask inside, who can join the work team and help with this?"* A five-year-old part volunteered, as she had spent much of her time as a child socializing. With the addition of the five-year-old and her social energy, Dora's work team was able to manage the social aspects and tasks of work. Note: The five-year-old did not come out at work but assisted from inside.

Example: Ann developed a work team and other parts agreed to not go to work. In exchange, Ann agreed to play "Candy Land", (a game she loathed, and they loved) for 20 minutes every day after work. One day she *"forgot,"* and the next day child parts showed up at work. The agreement was quickly reaffirmed.

Example: Robert worked as a ground's keeper for a facility. He never went inside as child parts were afraid of being trapped. The parts were oriented to the present and an agreement was made that Robert would take care of work and the parts could stay in their safe spaces. Eventually, Robert got many promotions and ended up running a department in the same facility.

Parenting Teams: Mothers and Fathers and Caretakers with DID

All of the following recommendations need to be negotiated with as much of the system as possible, and periodically need to be reviewed to see if they are working or need to be adjusted.

Developing Parenting Teams (consolidated notes from Gloria Rodberg's 2005 ISSTD annual conference presentation)

- Identify parts who have the ability to parent and those who do not. Create a parenting team if necessary. (Division of labour, like who drives and who doesn't)
- Make agreements on who should be out with the children, who can be out with supervision of the adult

parenting parts, and parts who should have limited or no contact with the children.
- Monitor agreements and review them to see if anything needs to be added or adjusted.
- C ontract with all parts that external children will be protected, will not be hurt or have their needs neglected. This mirrors goals of internal parenting and caretaking among parts.
- Problem Solve, e.g., what to do if a child part pops out with an external child.
- Negotiate with potentially abusive and neglectful parts.
- Confront self-destructive and substance abuse behavior around external children.
- Limit the number of parent parts out with children. (Research indicates that less is better)
- Parts out with children should use the adult voice to decrease confusion.
- Clarify positive benefits of the parenting agreement.

Example: Sarah had teen parts that resented her children and liked going out drinking. Sarah was angry at the teens for risking her being reported to the state for child neglect, and for driving drunk. The teen parts reasoned that the children weren't theirs, so they didn't have to parent, and initially refused to negotiate because they thought they would be forced to give up going out drinking. Once enough Self energy was reached among parts, Sarah and the teens could have curiosity about and listen to each other. Sarah pointed out that if she got reported to the state, she would be very sad which would make the body feel heavy and have no energy. The teens hated the way the body felt when Sarah was sad but did not want to stop going out. An agreement was reached that Sarah would get a babysitter once/week so the teens could go out and drink if they agreed to not drink dangerously, and to travel by cab.

People with DID have a range of ability to parent and our job is to support them in doing the best job possible.

Kluft's study (1987) of 75 mothers in treatment for DID resulted in 38 % being competent parents, 16% abusive and 45 % having difficulty. If necessary, children should be periodically assessed to evaluate if they are being adversely affected by their parents.

As with all clients, therapists must know and be able to follow the regulations of reporting allegations or instances of child abuse and neglect to their state office. For one thing, it is the law. For another, if you don't report, it replicates the childhoods of our clients in that no one noticed or took steps to stop abuse that was happening.

Other Team Examples

The following are examples of different occasions where team development was useful.

Example: A client needed to get a colonoscopy and was very triggered. After negotiating, it was decided two of the older parts would manage the appointment while the rest of the parts would avoid the whole procedure by staying in my office.

Example: Mary had child parts who liked coming out and playing with her children. What they gained was the ability to have a safe experience of play. These parts did not have the skills to manage situations where an adult was needed, and spoke like small children. Resolution was that the child parts could come out and play with the external children under the supervision of Mary or another parenting part. Child parts agreed to use Mary's voice when speaking to the children to decrease confusion.

Example: Tom had a part who had flashbacks whenever his son (age 2) said "No." He would see his son as a *"giant who is going* *to beat me up*". He was reported to the state for abusing his son and referred for therapy. The part who had flashbacks when his son said "No" was helped to develop a container for old traumatic material and a safe space. The agreement was that whenever Tom was with his son, that part would stay in his safe space. Tom was grateful for the help. He said, had he known help was available, he would have gotten it a long time ago.

Example: One part of a complex system handled the client's work in a hospital. This work part did not have anything to do with the rest of the client's life and was not directly involved with therapy as it was critical for the client to keep functioning at work. This part did benefit indirectly from therapy. As parts were worked with, the work part became more assertive at work . The plan was to do all the trauma work we could with the rest of the system, and then work on whatever the work part needed. Unfortunately, a series of events required the client to drop out of treatment before that could happen. Fortunately, she had made enough progress that she continued to be less symptomatic and have an easier life.

Summary

Teaching clients to negotiate and develop teams is a skill that can be used whenever necessary. Some teams function for a long time, and some may be developed for a single event. All teams need to be negotiated and developed with the agreement of as much of the system as possible and need to be periodically reviewed to see if the team is working or needs to be adjusted. Teams often need to be adjusted as progress is made. Teamwork is helpful in managing daily life, and the process of developing and using teams helps clients increase integrated functioning.

Section 3.
Orienting Parts to the Present, also Known as Retrieval

Introduction

This section will address:
- What happens when a part does not want to be retrieved?
- What happens when exiles block access to Self and witnessing?
- What happens when the burdens of exiles are causing excess overwhelm and anxiety?
- What happens when exiles and other parts are locked into believing they live in the past?
- Different strategies of orienting/retrieval.

Multiple Reality Disorder

Managers, firefighters, and exiles all live lives that are more or less influenced and defined by their childhoods. Parts for people with dissociative disorders are more *"cut off from full memory and pensive self-observation, (and thus they) remain prone to react in their specialized patterns."* (Kluft,1993) Kluft refers to this as Multiple Reality Disorder, as some parts will be living in the present, some parts will be totally immersed in the past, and some will fluidly live in different time zones. *"...the various alters (parts), working from different assumptions, drawing upon different databases, and thinking with different cognitive schemes and patterns, live in different subjective realities."* (Kluft, 1993 p. 147)

Phase One: Establishing the Treatment, Developing Coping and Stabilization Skills

It is difficult to fully appreciate the tenacity of "multiple reality disorder" even in clients who have been in treatment for extended periods of time. My appreciation of this was heightened by a child part in a complex system that had already done much successful trauma work. In my office this part knew the correct year and that her home and my office were in Massachusetts, yet when she walked into the waiting room, she felt instantly back in her past and original home state where she experienced abuse every day. This belief caused her to feel considerably at risk of danger from the past and led her to block present efforts to process traumatic material. Following this experience, I began looking closely for these discrepancies and have used this intervention with the goal of reducing anxiety and increasing clients' ability to differentiate the past from the present. Another important point is that parts who are oriented to the present may periodically slide back into the past until they are fully unburdened. They will, however, be easier to reorient.

Clients with dissociative disorders and complex PTSD may have parts who are not able to learn coping skills, be witnessed and/or unburdened, until they are retrieved/oriented to the present. Parts "living" in their childhood, experiencing the felt sense of being abused and neglected every day, may not believe it's safe to communicate or work on anything until they have been oriented to the present. Old messages including threats about what will happen if they tell and lies communicating that safety can only be found by following family rules, can be remarkably tenacious. In addition, adult parts of the system may not want exiles in the present because of fear (or the reality) that they may be too disruptive.

Example: When trying to retrieve one of Buck's parts, the part stated that he was not allowed to leave home, or he would be beaten. He was unable to do any witnessing because of his belief that if he told anyone anything, he and his little brother would both be beaten. Buck also did not want this exile to join him in the present as the exile had a history of anxiety.

Timing of Teaching Orienting Strategies

It is important to attend to the timing and use of these techniques. Although these techniques do not interfere with the dissociation of traumatic material, they do increase a system's overall knowledge and awareness of the present. For some, this can cause distress. As Loewenstein (1993) pointed out, *"The selectively focused attention of the MPD (DID) patient often helps to maintain dissociation so intensely that any movement toward greater awareness may be experienced as dysphoric."* When such a dynamic is present, the use of these techniques must be postponed, and need to be done with more preparation.

Orienting Strategies

The strategies in this chapter all facilitate internal communication and cooperation, decrease anxiety, increase grounding in the present, and can help decrease some negative transferences. They can be done with slow bilateral tapping which is an EMDR adaptation (See Chapter 9 for a text box on Bilateral Tapping) that is easy for anyone to use. In my experience, this helps facilitate internal communication. This process also works without bilateral communication as parts being addressed will be more likely to be listening and taking in information. Because much of the therapy will be done through direct access, orienting provides parts who have little to no connection with Self with evidence outside of the rigid options and beliefs from the past.

7 Steps to Differentiate the Past from the Present
(Twombly, J. 2000)

1. Beginning with parts (often Managers) who are oriented to the present, discuss all or some of the following and make a list of:
   a. How do they know what year it is? (e.g., calendar date)
   b. How many years has it been since they were last abused?
   c. How have they organized their life so they are safe? e.g.,
      i. Where do they live,
      ii. How do they know their partner, roommate, etc. does not abuse them,
      iii. Where is their place of work, car ownership, etc.

> Note: With dissociative disordered clients, child parts do not always function like children and

> may have adult skills. Thus, child parts may be the managers and be oriented to the present.

Identifying concrete differences between the past and the present helps the parts differentiate the past from present. In addition to a verbal list of the differences, I suggested that the information be visualized in pictures and videos. Thus, the adult might identify the location of their current home verbally, with a visualized detailed picture, and with a fast-forward visualized video of their history in the house from when they moved in to the present. Visual information helps extend communication to nonverbal parts and adds a timespan dimension that increases the credibility of communications. At times, information gathered needs to be adjusted to the targeted parts. For instance, child parts may respond more fully to child types of observations. One client's list included that child parts could have cocoa whenever they wanted. This was symbolic of how their wishes and needs were heard and responded to now versus in the past.

2. Request that the part or parts to whom the information is directed be open to receiving it, without the expectation that they believe it.

   Example: *Could Gale and Jess be open to listening and watching the information Sari is going to give you? You don't have to believe her, just take it in. Once you've received it, you can ask any questions you have. When you leave here, please check out the information for yourselves. Next week it will be interesting to hear what you agree or disagree with. Do you have any questions before we start?*

   Arguments about veracity are minimized by not expecting belief. An alternative, with the advantage of extending the potential impact of the exercise is to make the statement more inclusive, e.g., *"Could Gale and Jess and anyone else who needs this information…"*

At times, it is not clear what part of the dissociated system will be receiving the information. In this case, the instruction is more general. For example, say: *Would parts please be open to listening, watching and taking in this information? You don't need to believe it. You can ask questions and check it out later.*

3. Ask the adult and/or other oriented parts to visualize sending/broadcasting the information to parts that are to receive it, or simply to all parts of the mind.

4. Ask the adult and/or other oriented parts how the process went. Sometimes, parts will add more items to the list.
5. Ask parts who received the information if they have any questions. It is common for parts to verbalize disbelief or to feel "tricked." Alternatively, they might feel some cautious relief.
6. Homework

7. Homework consists of parts checking out the information with the adult and/or other oriented parts supporting that process by pointing out concrete detailed evidence, e.g., *Here is our white house with the green shutters (not the brick one we grew up in). Notice all the Massachusetts license plates (not the Maine ones where we grew up.)*
8. 7. Follow up in the next session.

> Note: If you are using bilateral tapping, there are two possibilities. 1. Have the oriented part tap in the list after each number, or 2. Tap continuously until the whole list is finished. Tapping is always done slowly as fast tapping can bring up traumatic material.

Example: A client entered treatment for a long-term anxiety disorder which had not been helped by previous long-term treatment. Once diagnosed with DID, it was clear that most parts thought they were still living in the 1970s, in the home where they grew up, being abused and terrorized. Her list of differences between her childhood and the present included:

1. A fast-forward video from when she was last abused at 17 and living at home, to college, to the present. It included different apartments she had lived in, and that she had now lived in her house for 5 years.
2. A fast-forward video of her partner from meeting him to the present, and the information that he had never hit or abused her.
3. That her dog Skippy was 3 years old, and an image of herself and Skippy playing Frisbee (something she did not do with her childhood dog)
4. That she had a job and a blue Toyota hatchback.

5. That she now lives in Massachusetts not where she grew up in Iowa, a map image of where Iowa and her childhood home was, where her current home is, and how long it would take to walk from her current home to Iowa (sounds funny but this had an impact on the child part).
6. An image of her mother, how she looks now, and where she lives.
7. That her father got sick with cancer, got progressively sicker and weaker, and died in 1990. She included where he was buried and images from the funeral.

Example: A 41-year-old client in process of taking his first college class in 20 years noted that he was having trouble completing a take home exam. Asking inside yielded the information that a part was preventing him from taking it to protect him from his mother's savage criticism. The adult part identified concrete evidence of how his mother had changed in that now she showed interest in his class work and praised his good grades. This information and visualizations of these interactions were then communicated to the part. The adult reported that the part argued but then agreed to let him complete one take-home exam once as a trial experience. The part, age 12, then came out, agreed to check out the mother's reactions for himself, and began yawning and feeling waves of fatigue. He explained that for the first time ever, he felt he could relax.

Example: A client with a childhood history of many traumatic surgeries began orienting parts to the present and suddenly smelled ether, an anaesthetic agent. This indicated that some child parts believed they lived in the hospital. After reminding parts that there was no expectation of belief and requesting that they simply take in the information, the client was able to communicate her list of differentiations between the past and present to the parts. In between sessions, the client called to report that they had awakened the next morning smelling ether, went through the whole process again by asking parts inside to watch while they walked around their apartment showing them locked windows and doors, and introducing the parts to their dog. (Note: walking is another form of bilateral stimulation.) By the next session, they reported that they could now see her apartment more completely, realized they had always viewed their home in sections as if they had been wearing blinders, and noted their general anxiety level had decreased.

Example: A married woman's child parts believed that their life was as dangerous as their childhood had been, because they could not say "no" when their husband wanted sex and he did not listen to her. The client made a list that differentiated the present from her very abusive childhood. It included that she was working and saving money in a secret bank account to move out, and that although she couldn't say "No" when her husband wanted sex, he did not want sex more than once a week, and there was never any bleeding afterwards.

Example: A client, abused on a beach during childhood, became suddenly anxious and physically weak during a walk on a beach. As no parts responded when he asked inside about the cause, he made an educated guess that there was at least one part of him who was confusing the past with the present. After stating that concerned parts did not have to believe him and requesting that they just listen and watch, he communicated the following statements and pictures: how this beach looked different from the one in the past, that his abusive father had been dead for 25 years, a picture of their last sight of him before he died, and a view of his grave site. He immediately felt relief and was able to continue his walk

> Note: As in the above example, clients are encouraged to try using this technique on their own when they are triggered by reminders of their past. Obviously, this technique requires at least one part that is grounded in present reality. Persons for whom this technique has not worked have been poorly grounded overall, and lacked parts who could reasonably identify facts about the present.

Example: A woman was referred after being destabilized in her prior treatment. She spent many hours in bed and her home was a mess. Parts said they didn't trust her because she was so disabled. I said, "It's true that she is disabled, but she is still keeping you safer than any day in your childhood, plus she is working with me on getting to know all of you and healing. After this communication, parts were more willing to engage in treatment.

Height Orientation (Twombly, J. 2000)

Orientation, usually thought of in terms of time (past vs. present), can be applied to height (short vs. tall). For the most part, child parts experience themselves as child sized. Orientation to height can lessen anxiety and give child parts another experience of how the present is very different from the past.

Ask a child part to volunteer to try an experiment or to be co-conscious with an adult part and experience the exercise through their connection with the adult part. Ask the part to see how high they can reach something, for instance, on the top shelf of a bookcase. Child parts tend to be extremely surprised when they can easily reach much higher than expected. The awareness can be installed with bilateral tapping, or by having the client just feel into the awareness of adult height and communicate it to all parts.

Orienting to Height

How high up can you reach on that door or bookcase? Check it out!
Ask all the parts who are willing, to check it out.
Install awareness (butterfly hug, tapping).
Check it out on other doors.

Note: BEING tall doesn't mean you can drive - have to be over 16 and know how to drive safely!

Responses to height orientation can be idiosyncratic. One part wondered if the bookshelf had been shrunk by magic. Also, the part's perceived age does not appear to change with their altered perception of body height.

Obviously, this technique is not appropriate for parts who believe that growing up or being large is in some way dangerous, therefore the timing of its use has to be evaluated. In addition, child parts who are very dissociated may not be able to reach higher than the dictates of their perceived height.

Example: A child part, despite appearing fully oriented to the present, believed that she was trapped in my office and that she was too small to reach and unlock the door (which was, in fact, not locked). With some encouragement, she managed to tolerate her terror enough to be able to test out how high she could reach. She was astonished to find out she could reach all the way to the top of the door and open it easily. The awareness of her ability was installed, and for homework, she was asked to check out all the doors in her home and to learn, assisted by older parts, how to lock and unlock them. This was particularly important for this client who as a child had been too short to unlock a door to escape the room in which she was being abused.

Example: In preparation for trauma work, it was decided to try to orient a group of anxious young parts to their current height. With much trepidation a child part volunteered to try first and was surprised to see he could easily reach higher than the top of a door. He then exclaimed that the therapist looked short to him for the very first time. This knowledge of height was installed and communicated systemwide. The adult/daily life team and several parts reported that their overall anxiety was reduced significantly.

> Note: We found it necessary to ask the adult/daily life team to renew some limits with these parts, since some felt being tall meant they could drive and come out at work.

Example: A client had to travel by air and was very afraid. We discovered that their idea of air travel was that they would be trapped on a plane full of tall adult men smoking cigars. We oriented them to their height, and then to my height, since both the client and I were tall. The flight went well, and there was increased comfort in working with me because the perceived height difference (which I had not been aware of) was corrected.

Orienting to the Therapist and Therapist's Office (Twombly, J. 2000)

I began using this technique when I became aware that many parts were coming to sessions, checking me out as if they had never met me. Orienting to the therapist and therapist's office appears to help clients and their systems of parts accrue information and increase cooperation with the therapist. It is clear that DID clients' transference reactions are complicated and vary among personality states. Lowenstein (1993) described often covert "...negative transference concerns about the therapist's trustworthiness, inherent dangerousness, and potential abusiveness." This technique can help to at least minimize some of these negative transferences.

Specifically, when the client has had enough experience with the therapist and therapist's office, it is helpful to list and communicate concrete knowledge and observations to any parts willing to accept the information. Parts are then asked to keep watching the therapist, keep gathering information, and keep testing the therapist's trustworthiness.

The following information is helpful to be aware of, observe, communicate and discuss:

1. Factual information about the appearance of the office, including orientation information such as a current year calendar or modern computer.
2. Safety oriented information, e.g.,
    - That the client sits on a chair across from where the therapist sits.
    - Circumstances of any physical contact between the therapist and client (e.g., a handshake).
    - That abuse is not allowed in the office and has never happened.

- And any information a particular client might need. E.g., one client was worried someone was hiding in the closet. They checked the closet to find that no one was in the closet, and this fact was included in the information about the therapist's office.
3. The following significant interactions are helpful to note and communicate:
   - When the client got angry, the therapist responded non-punitively.
   - When the therapist went on vacation, he/she returned.
   - Any and all disagreements that were worked out.
   - That there were numerous occasions when the therapist was empathic and nothing bad happened.
4. The therapist's appearance, voice, and any other identifying information that's relevant.
5. A fast-forward video spanning the treatment from beginning to the present.

Example: The information in this example was quite tentative. A client of 8 years could identify only that the therapist had never yelled at, laughed at, hurt her, or used anything she had said against her. Parts who received the information then argued that the therapist was still dangerous because some of the people who had hurt them had "acted nice" at first. The adult and therapist managed to identify one important difference—the people who had hurt her had "acted nice" for only short amounts of time, while the therapist had been "acting nice" for eight years. This difference was communicated verbally and with a fast-forward video of the eight-year treatment process, along with encouragement to keep watching and checking the therapist out.

Example: A client with little internal communication suddenly said they had a "weird sense of not being sure" they were in the therapist's office or somewhere else. After installing and communicating a quick review of weekly sessions for the past two years, plus how this therapist differed from the previous therapist, (the current therapist's voice was more confident, and she was taller), this client felt grounded.

Example: A client's father had abused him sadistically. During witnessing, he said, "Your face just turned into my father's. Keep talking." Because my voice had been included in the information about me that was communicated to all parts, he was able to continue the witnessing process.

Orienting a Part to the Adult Within the System of Parts

When a part does not trust the adult in the system, does not believe the adult can handle any or enough painful feelings, or protect the system, ask the part to look in the eyes of the adult and ask the adult to look into the eyes of the child. Have the adult communicate their age and any other information the child needs to know to begin to trust the adult enough. One thing that is always important for the adult to communicate is that the adult has skills and resources he/she/they did not have as a child. The child part can then ask any questions they have.

Phase One: Establishing the Treatment, Developing Coping and Stabilization Skills

Example: A part blocked witnessing an exile's burden. The concern was that the client/adult could not handle witnessing any of the burden the exile was carrying. The blocking part was asked to look in the adult's eyes while the adult looked back into the blocking part's eyes and communicated her age, skills, work in therapy, and that their parents were dead. The blocking part was assured that the adult could handle the witnessing.

Example: A part scathingly referred to the adult as useless and totally untrustworthy. The parts were asked to look at look in the eyes of the adult and that the adult to look in the eyes of the parts. The adult told the parts that although their life was a dysfunctional mess, she was still taking better care of them than they were taken care of any day in her childhood, plus they were working with me and making slow but steady progress.

Another strategy is to have the adult ask the part(s) to look through his/her/their eyes and check out the therapy office and the therapist, and to ask any questions they have. This can also be adapted to work during sessions via Zoom or another remote platform.

Strategy: For Clients with No Oriented Parts
(Fisher, J. in Twombly, J. 2000)

This protocol is very useful for clients who seem to have no oriented parts and/or whose rapid switching makes therapy difficult. Fisher recommends standing up with the client using bilateral movement (e.g., stepping from one foot to the other). The bilateral movement is mirrored by the therapist who speaks continuously orienting the client with some repetitive combination of: *"I want all of you to be present in my office, and all of you to look through the eyes and notice what it's like... you can tell you're in my office because there's the* (mention concrete details), *and we're both here together, and in this moment in time nothing bad is happening... I want all of you to feel the feeling of your feet on the ground, your ankles, your legs, the feel of your clothes and want all of you to look around and see you're right here in my office, it's* (state the year), *and in this moment in time everything's ok, just keep looking around and see what it's like to be here in my office, notice that nothing bad is happening right now... Notice if you feel any tension, you can put your attention on it and let it come up and go by, just notice* (increasing mindfulness)...

It is recommended that you do this exercise with the client for 5-10 minutes every session (usually this depends on what the client can tolerate) until enough parts are oriented enough to begin to learn other coping strategies. Although the recommendation is to stand up with the client and use bilateral movement, bilateral tapping can also be used. I do not stand up with my clients as I am much taller than most of them.

This protocol helps disoriented clients' systems begin to become oriented and grounded, and helps develop systemwide awareness of the present. After a few sessions, one client who had very little connection with her system and had argued that no place was safe, began to feel more settled in my office, noticed more of her parts were present, and began to have communication with more parts in her system.

Strategy: Identifying Feelings That Belong to the Past

When clients (or parts) are feeling a strong negative emotion or cluster of emotions, I ask them to

1. Lightly focus on the feeling in their body, and to
2. Notice what % of the feeling belongs to the past.

Once the percentage is identified, it is often helpful to put that % in a container. (See Chapter 4)

This exercise is assisted by hypnotic language. Using words used by the client and the suggestion to focus on the feeling in their body facilitates the trance they are already in. This is followed by the positive suggestion of "Notice what % belongs to the past ." Most clients and parts come up with a concrete percentage, and for the rest, it is easy to identify that at least much of it comes from the past. If a client says, "None of it comes from the past, it's all about now." I say, *"That's not mathematically possible, as there was a lot of hopelessness in your childhood, and we haven't finished working on it. So, the old hopelessness blends with the today hopelessness and makes it feel worse than it needs to be."*

This exercise helps clients differentiate which feelings are about the present and which come from the past. As with all interventions, they must be used with clinical judgement and adjusted to meet specific client needs. Even if a client cannot put the old percentage in a container, the knowledge that an amount of the feelings belongs to the past is helpful.

Example: A client came in feeling "hopeless" and "helpless" about her daughter's recent cancer diagnosis and treatment. I said,

"*Focus lightly on the hopeless and helpless feelings in your body... What % of them belongs to your childhood?*" She said 70 percent. I said, "How about if we put that 70% in a container. We will work on them when the time is right and having them stored will help you be able to support your daughter and manage today easier."

Example: A client was furious with her wife and thinking about divorce. I asked her to focus on the furious feelings in her body and she identified 90 % came from her childhood. I suggested she put the divorce on hold until we had more of a chance to deal with the old fury. This exercise helped her identify which feelings were old and which were present day. Arguments with her wife became more constructive.

Example: A man had trouble dealing with his critical boss. It made him depressed and anxious. It was much easier to deal with his legitimately difficult boss after he had put the 60% of the depressed/angry feelings from his past into a container.

Example: A couple with a volatile relationship worked with a couple's therapist and learned to use time outs when they got into clashes. When they used the time outs, each was instructed to ask themselves what % of the feelings came from the past. The couple noted that the old feelings threw gas on their current disagreements making them much harder to deal with.

Summary of Different Strategies to Orient Parts

- To the present
- To height
- To the therapist
- Child part to the adult in the system
- Protocol for clients with no oriented parts
- Daily homework
- Percentage of feeling that has to do with now, percentage of the feeling that has to do with the past

CHAPTER 12

Phase 2: IFS Witnessing and Unburdening: Paced, Protective and Productive Working Through of Traumatic Material

Introduction

Before beginning Phase Two with clients, ensure that they have been practicing and managing their symptoms during the week. Ideally, they will come in reporting experiences like, *"I got triggered at work, went to the ladies' room, did some Safe Space Imagery and felt grounded enough to keep working."* Or, *"A part got afraid when they saw a guy who looked like our father. I reminded her he's dead, and we put the fear in the container."* Or *"I got my car and was too little to drive. I sat there with my hands on the wheel and asked the part to let the adult me drive so we could go home."*

Beginning Phase 2 is not recommended when the following is true:

1. The client does not have the ego strengths or is too fragile.
2. The therapist will be transferring the client. For example, a consultee who was retiring in several months, took on a client with DID. She contracted with the client to work on Phase One only.

3. A client is too unstable. Use clinical judgement. For example, I once began Phase 2 with a client who became unstable as we touched on traumatic material. We immediately returned to Phase 1 and stayed mostly there with only gentle forays into Phase 2. Another example is a client with bipolar disorder and a trauma history. She went into a manic phase which delayed beginning phase 2.

Paced Processing of Traumatic Material

The goal is to be able to process, witness and unburden traumatic material while the client continues to be stable, and have control and choices. I often say, *"You didn't have control or choices during your childhood, you need to have control and choices over your healing."* When clients have concerns that this phase might take forever or be impossible. I tell them, *"Our childhoods didn't last forever, so this trauma work can't last forever either." "And, you got through your childhood all by yourself, we are two adults here, we should be able to get you through your healing."* Another concern is whether every single traumatic event has to be individually processed. I assure clients, *"Child abuse is often repetitive, so we'll just work on representative examples and then can easily finish off any loose ends from similar events."*

The witnessing of traumatic material needs to be paced, so the client can continue to function during the week. For the most part, if the client is not functioning or functioning well enough during the week, it is necessary to return to Phase 1 and figure out what needs to happen to return to the trauma work with adequate stability.

Example: A client began to get destabilized while witnessing a traumatic event. The therapist thought continuing with the witnessing the event would help. The client got more and more destabilized.

Choosing the First Target

The goal of working on the first target is to develop a system of working together so witnessing and unburdening can be accomplished while the client maintains their level of functioning and progress is made. Therefore, I work with the client to pick a target that ideally only happened once and isn't connected to other targets. For example: a client was raped by family members for much of her childhood. We chose to start with a date rape in high school versus the family abuse because it only happened once. Often it is helpful to begin with a manager held target/burden. This has the advantage of strengthening the manager who can then help other parts with their witnessing.

Sessions where the goal is witnessing trauma should follow Kluft's "rule of thirds" (Kluft, 1993): Spend the first third of the session setting up the trauma work, the second third doing it, and the final third talking about the work and making sure the client leaves the session stable. It can be exciting when a client is making progress in a session, but any progress you make may be erased if you do not leave enough time at the end of the session to stabilize the client and avoid backlash.

> **Length and Frequency of Sessions**
>
> Most often I work in sessions that run from 45 minutes to 1 hour and 20 minutes, one to two times per week. Ideally, the length and frequency are based on the client's clinical needs and preferences. Too often, however, it is determined by the dictates of a client's insurance company when the client does not have the ability to self-pay. One client, for example, could only afford to see me every other week.

> It is ALWAYS important to follow Kluft's rule of thirds since every client has a different tolerance level. It is especially important when sessions are shorter and less frequent, however, to evaluate how much trauma work can be accomplished without putting undo stress on the client.

Using Titration to Process and Witness Trauma (adapted from Twombly, 2005)

As Kluft said, the goal is to titrate trauma work into manageable amounts. The following example includes many options for titrating. It is an example of working with a client who had a history of suicide attempts, multiple hospitalizations and self-mutilation. She had coping skills and used them but having been in prior treatment that eroded her dissociative defenses she remained at risk of destabilization. The more risk the client has of losing control, the more control I build in.

Example: While working with this client, we identified an initial trauma that happened only once and named it Trauma X. All the other burdens were put in a large container while Trauma X was put in a separate container. Next the client and I decided to put ten % of Trauma X into a smaller container. Then we identified which parts were involved in Trauma X and needed to be present for the witnessing. Three parts were involved and these became the "work group." Because this client's system was large enough, we identified a "helper part" who was willing to help with the witnessing.

In this model, all parts who are not either directly involved or being witnessed are asked to go to their safe spaces with sound- and feeling-proofing in the walls (Twombly 2005). Parts who handle daily life activities like work and parenting are also asked to go to

Phase 2: IFS Witnessing and Unburdening

their safe spaces to be protected from the impact of witnessing as they need to continue to function (Fine 1993).

> Feeling-proofing is something I began adding to Soundproofing as it occurred to me that it would be useful. Because clients with complex trauma disorders are often in trance these kinds of suggestions are easy to incorporate.

The working group was asked to have one part speak for all (a "spokes-part"). This spokes-part is checked for enough Self energy in relation to the work group.

The work group was asked to go to a safe room with a TV. They used the remote to turn the TV to a channel that showed the work group, me, and the helper part present in my office. They practiced turning the TV on and off until they felt they had practiced enough. Notice how much control is built into this process—the parts can turn the TV on and off, and the picture on the TV is one with me supporting them in the present.

Next, they were asked to turn the Picture within the Picture (PIP) (a small screen in the bottom right corner of the TV screen) to something benign. They chose a sailboat and practiced turning that on and off. The PIP is where the trauma work is done while the whole screen remains on the picture of the client and me in the present or if the client prefers, to something benign (for example, the client may prefer to have something like roses or a sail boat on the big screen instead).

Trauma and Dissociation Informed Internal Family Systems

When the work group felt in control of turning the TV on and off and the PIP on and off, I asked the helper to ask the work group to take 2 seconds of traumatic material out of the small container and let me know when they had it/felt it. Then it was witnessed for 2 seconds while I counted out loud. Then the work group was reminded by the helper and me to put what was left back in the container. Then I asked what was witnessed and they reported, "2 seconds of terror."

The helper and the work group agreed it had gone well, and with the same procedure, witnessed 2 more seconds. After that they decided to try 5 seconds. Three sets of 5 seconds were done, and then they decided try 10 seconds. The trauma was put back in the container after each set of witnessing.

Once the work group and the helper felt comfortable, the witnessing looked more like typical witnessing with the only difference being that it was returned to the container each time.

Once the witnessing part of the session was done the work group was asked what they were noticing. They expressed that they felt lighter and that some of the burdens had been lifted. I then asked if they wanted to invite any other positive qualities in besides the lightness and they said they just wanted to rest in their safe space and play. The helper also went to her safe space to rest.

Other parts were asked to return from their safe spaces and I told them it had gone well and the work team and helper were resting in their safe spaces. The other parts wanted to know what we worked on and I said, "*We worked on the target and will continued the process next week.*" To specifically answer that question would have led to potential overwhelm and disrupting the pacing of this careful process.

The target was finished over the next two sessions. This is an example of a process with a lot of titration, control, and choices. The parts were happy because they had never been able to work on any trauma because when they did (in previous treatment) they got overwhelmed and suicidal. The witnessing itself is done either with the assistance of a part (or parts) who has enough Self energy (perhaps a manager) and who was not involved with the event. Or by the working group who have enough control via the system we set up. Once the event is fully witnessed and the exiles unburdened, information about the event will automatically become available to the adult/Self-like parts (Fine 1991).

Example: One man had C-PTSD from a reaction to a drug he had taken recreationally that was so traumatic, he was terrified to work on it. With this process, he was able to have control, face the witnessing (starting with 2 seconds then increasing the amount of time) and unburden the drug reaction in one session.

Example: This example is of a later target, witnessed once initial targets were witnessed and unburdened. The client could only tell me that the trauma we were working on involved four kinds of screaming and that she felt too much shame to tell me anything more. She took an Ativan before we began the trauma work which gave her an additional feeling of control. The work team and helper part put the four kinds of screaming in separate containers and she decided to start on the one containing her suppressed screams. We systematically worked through the contents of the containers in two sessions and then the client was able to tell me that the four kinds of screaming occurred when she was forced to abuse a smaller child. She had been told that she could "choose" to abuse him or be abused herself in a way more painful than ever. Before the witnessing she had felt responsible for her "choice." After we completed the process, she could see that her father had orchestrated the whole event and that she had had no choice.

When working with dissociative disordered clients, keep in mind that you never know exactly what is going on in the internal system. For example, while working with one client, we began working on a section and he suddenly said, *"There is a whole bunch of parts around that I don't know."* In this case, we created a safe space around the group and to ensure no parts but the working group would be impacted by the traumatic material, made a safe wall around the working group. Another example is when a "small" target turned into a very complex one. The complexity had been dissociated.

Example: A child part in the system of a complex DID client called me to tell me others were homicidal and had a gun. We contracted that they would leave the gun home and she came in for an emergency session. The adult in the system arrived for the session and said, *"I don't know why I'm here but I knew I had to come."* All parts except the parts who called me were asked to go to their safe spaces. The part who had called and two other nine-year-olds told me there was a group of homicidal parts and she was afraid that the adult would act on the homicidal impulses if she knew about the gun. We built a safe space around the homicidal parts that was so big they never reached the edges of it. The 3 nine-year-olds had enough Self energy to take a "handful" of traumatic material from the homicidal parts and witness it. A "handful" may not sound like a lot, but it was agonizing material. We were able to systematically witness all of it over three extended sessions. As the

Phase 2: IFS Witnessing and Unburdening

traumatic material was witnessed and unburdened, the homicidal parts in their safe space became less active and eventually calmer, and the nine-year-olds felt more confident and solid. During this work, the adult who was protected from the witnessing, was able to continuing working. Once the witnessing was finished and the trauma unburdened, the information automatically became available to the adult.

Comment:

This is an example of trauma work done towards the end of this client's therapy. She had already made enormous amounts of progress witnessing and unburdening traumas. This material had been triggered by her witnessing a fist fight during a bad break up. Later I found out there was no actual gun which was a huge relief to me.

This process may sound unwieldy, but it made it possible to safely witness horrific abuse.

Summary of Protected Steps for IFS Unburdening/Processing of Traumatic Material

1. When choosing an initial target, I recommend starting with a manager-held target that is an isolated or relatively recent traumatic event. The goal is to start with something that allows the client to have a successful experience of witnessing and gives you and the client a chance to practice working together on an easier target before undertaking more complex ones. One client chose to work on a bad experience she had at work, another chose being beaten up in high school, and another chose a memory of her father beating her dog to death. As these incidents were not repeated events, it was possible to finish working on them in one session, allowing the client to develop a sense of mastery.

2. Check for concerns. The client's system needs to be assured that all concerns will be addressed before any trauma work is done.
3. Organize the client's system so the client can be maintained at their highest level of functioning. One strategy is to initially protect the adult or team of parts who manage daily life from the impact of the trauma work. This is done by having the host or daily life team/managers go to their safe spaces and put sound- and feeling-proofing up. Once a target is processed, the information in its processed form will eventually get to the host/daily life managers. (Fine 1991). All parts not involved in the processing also are in their safe spaces.

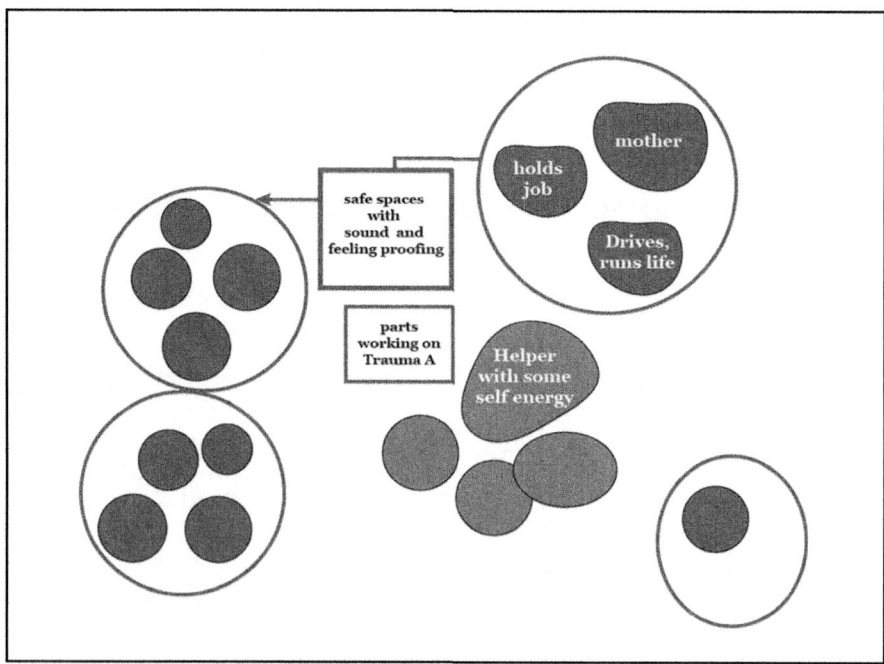

If parts handling daily life are not willing or able to work this way, witnessing needs to be done more carefully to protect stability.

Phase 2: IFS Witnessing and Unburdening

In this case, it is still often possible to minimize the number of other parts present by having any parts not needed for the targeted witnessing to go to their safe spaces and put sound- and feeling-proofing up. These safe spaces protect the parts who are not involved from getting destabilized during the witnessing.

Example: Concerns that a group of small parts would become triggered listening to a group of older parts working on graphic memories of a gang rape led to having the small parts go to their safe spaces. We put up sound- and feeling-proofing so they could be protected from hearing anything or experiencing any of the feelings from the older group. The older parts could then be witnessed and eventually unburdened.

4. Put all other traumatic material in a container (or several containers) with the commitment to working on the stored material when the time is right.
5. Put the target in a separate container.
6. Titrate the target, i.e., decide with parts what segment of the target to work on first. Possibilities include a % of affect, chunk of knowledge, sensation, or number of parts present. Limiting amount of material available is a way of helping the client maintain stability and control. I often start with 2 seconds of traumatic material, increasing the amount of time as the client's or group of parts' confidence grows. For some clients this amount of titration is provides enough protection and control that all targets can be witnessed.

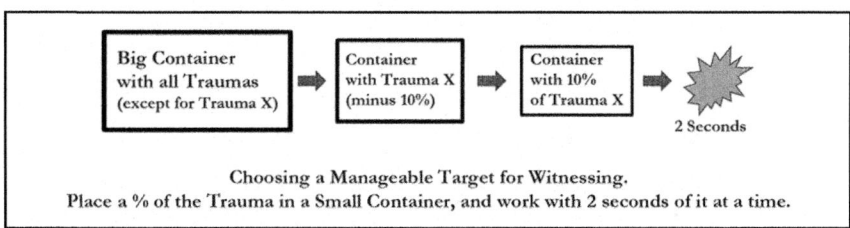

Choosing a Manageable Target for Witnessing.
Place a % of the Trauma in a Small Container, and work with 2 seconds of it at a time.

7. The more unstable a client is, the more coping skills and control I build in. Some clients need to use every part of this process, i.e., the TV and PIP, traumatic material being in containers, etc. and some can manage with less.
8. Make adjustments wherever necessary. Example: As the part with some self energy began witnessing, there was a rush of overwhelming anxiety. Focusing on the anxiety and asking the involved parts to relax back, we discovered 2 unidentified parts that needed safe spaces. Once that was done, we could continue.

    Example: As a client did his first 2 seconds, the PIP expanded to fill the whole screen. We reinforced the edges of the PIP so the traumatic material was contained.
9. Once the 2 seconds of witnessing is done, the part(s) puts remaining material back in the container. Ideally, the parts remember to do this, or can be reminded by me or the helper part (if one is identified).
10. When the witnessing and unburdening of the target section of the session is done, positive feelings can be invited in, or will just be evident. Sometimes the target will take more than one session and any unfinished traumatic material will need to be stored back in the container.
11. Then ask the parts what they need in between this session and the next. Sometimes it helps for the parts who worked during the session to rest in their safe spaces. Sometimes they want to do Deep Dreamless Sleep (see Chapter 4), or something else.
12. Ask the other parts to come back from their safe spaces and see if they or any of the parts have any questions or concerns. Details of traumatic material worked on should not be discussed as this can disrupt stability. When asked for details, I've sometimes said, "*We worked on the trauma*

Phase 2: IFS Witnessing and Unburdening

we decided to work on, made progress and will continue next week."

13. The last part of the session needs to be focused on checking for client stability and planning the next session.

Example: Sally was a 35-year-old woman with DID with a history of several hospitalizations and suicide attempts. She had a complex system where several parts helped manage her full-time job and life (the daily life team). As we discussed how to begin trauma processing, a group of four 13-year-olds said they had something to work on that had only happened once. Two other parts who were not involved in the event, agreed to help. These helper parts had enough Self energy and agreed to let me know if something was going wrong. The daily life team and all the other parts agreed to go to safe spaces and put sound- and feeling-proofing up. We checked to make sure all other traumatic material was stored in a vault, and the 13-year-olds stored what they wanted to work on in a smaller vault. We decided to start by having the 13-year-olds take out 2 seconds of the traumatic material. They took out the 2 seconds (extreme anxiety), and I counted seconds out loud which helped them stay grounded. The helpers reminded the 13-year-olds to put the anxiety back in the vault. The helper parts and 13-year-olds then noticed that one of the 13-year-olds was too upset to continue. She went into her safe space. The three remaining 13-year-olds took out another 2 seconds of anxiety and this time when they put it back in the vault, the process went smoothly and was in control. They felt good that the helpers and I were supportive with the witnessing. Then they decided they could try 5 seconds of traumatic material. After doing an additional set of 5 seconds, the trauma and the helpers witnessing the 13-year-olds felt that what had been worked on could be unburdened into a shaft of golden light. Once that was done, they felt some relief and increased confidence.

Over time, the 13-year-olds took out larger amounts from the vault without getting overwhelmed and the helpers and I continued witnessing. As the witnessing progressed, the 13-year-olds felt heard and some of the material was spontaneously unburdened. The rest continued to be unburdened into the golden light. The traumatic material was about her father slowly beating her beloved pet to death and threatening her with the same should she tell any "secrets."

After the 13-year-olds were fully unburdened, they noticed lightness and a sense of ease. They were told they could take in other important feelings. They noticed they were feeling stronger, a certainty it was not their fault, and they saw an image of their pet in heaven forgiving and loving them. The 13 year old who had not been able to witness joined them, and suddenly the 3 parts became reconfigured into one stronger part who felt synergy and a new level of strength. She and the helper parts decided to rest in their safe spaces. I asked the daily life team to come out and I explained to them that the 13-year-olds had done great, had finished working on what had been planned, and had integrated into one 13-year old part. I reminded them that they would find out about the traumatic material when the time was right, and that the 13-year-old and helpers were resting in their safe spaces. The daily life team checked with other parts who all wanted to stay in their safe spaces. Next session, the primary adult part told me that she knew what we had worked on. She said that she felt sad thinking about it, but the event felt like it had happened a long time ago. The 13-year-old continued to feel strong and volunteered to help with witnessing other parts carrying burdens.

Example: Pat, a DID client in her 60s, had spent her lifetime obsessively taking care of others. She was blended with many parts who numbed her out and savagely criticized her. She also had parts who thought all abuse was her fault and a part who wanted her to just continue helping because it was easier. When she became ready to work on the underlying traumatic belief that she could not say "No," we asked all parts who did not need to be present to go to their safe spaces or anywhere else they wanted to be (many of her parts liked waiting in my waiting room). Concerns about working on the traumatic belief included that everyone would abandon her, people would hate her, people would talk about her, and God would hate her. We managed to negotiate doing some work with a part who held some of the burdens of old exhaustion and heavy expectations. Parts were reminded that they would continue to have control and choices over whether they helped others or said "No."

Our goal for the session was to free up some energy which they all needed. I told these parts that I wanted them to watch as Pat and I worked with the part and to let us know if any concerns came up. I also said that I would check in with them before the end of the session. With that, the parts relaxed back enough for Pat to feel some Self energy.

Initially, the part was concerned that she was the burden and would disappear if she let go of the old feelings. I had Pat tell her, *"Babies aren't born with burdens. These are acquired through experiences and relationships. Nothing that's helpful will be lost by unburdening old feelings and beliefs. You'll still be there and will have more energy."* The part continued to be concerned, so I suggested we start with her unburdening 5% of the burden to see how it felt. The part agreed. The part decided to dump buckets of old exhaustion and expectations into a river, but then was worried she would be polluting the river with toxins. I explained (my concept) that burdens are tangled up energy, that once she lets them go, the energy goes back to neutral. That reassured the part, and I had Pat tell the part, *"Notice you have just the right kind of bucket and you are next to just the right river."* Once the part filled the bucket, it was too heavy, so I suggested maybe another part could help her. The part noticed that another part with similar burdens was there with her. The two were able to dump several buckets of exhaustion and expectations in the water. Once the 5% was done, the parts noticed they felt lighter and Pat noticed the parts were now holding hands, feeling connected to each other. They wanted to continue and got rid of a large amount of the burdens. Less burdened by old exhaustion and expectation, the parts and Pat suddenly became able to look at some of the current ways she was "helping" others and began to realize that they could begin to prioritize. Another part jumped in saying it was too dangerous to say "No" to anything. I asked the part to look at Pat while Pat looked at her. Pat told the part how old she was, and that she had strengths and resources that she did not have as a child. The part countered that Pat's life was a mess. Pat agreed, but pointed out differences, e.g., that she did not live with her parents, that she was in treatment and working on making progress, and that she had a safe home for all of the parts. I checked in with all the other parts who had relaxed back and they all felt some relief and expressed cautious willingness to think about the possibility of deciding to cut down on more of the excessive helpfulness.

Titrating with Blocking Parts

Example: A client with enough Self energy (actually a Self-like part with enough Self energy) stated she felt *"nothing"* towards an exile. This indicated that a blocking part was present. I asked the part if she could feel some curiosity toward the blocking part and she could. I asked her to let the blocking part feel her curiosity, and to tell the blocking part, *"We will not work with the exile until the blocking part says it's ok."* Then she was instructed to ask the blocking part, *"What do you think would happen if you stopped blocking?"* The blocking part said, *"If I let any feelings through, you'll totally fall apart."* I said, *"Ask the blocking part how old she thinks you are?"* The part thought she was 10 and was still living in the past.

I said, *"Ask the part to look in your eyes and look back at her. Let the blocking part know how old you are and that you have strengths and resources you didn't have when you were 10."* The part was relieved, and then retrieved. Then we negotiated with the blocking part to allow ten % access to the exile and to stand by and cut off this access if the Self-like part got overwhelmed. .

In this example, the blocking part who had been blocking total access, was coached to upgrade its ability to block so it could open a window and allow ten % access, and then to shut it if necessary. This is an example of upgrading a dissociative defence so it became a help in the witnessing/unburdening process.

Comment: Other IFS like strategies for processing traumatic material include having a blocking or numbing part help by allowing only five % connection between self and the part with the burden. Again, it can help to have a large percentage of the burden put in a container to reduce the possibility of destabilizing the client.

Example: As a teenager, Ron had been raped by a charismatic man who manipulated and blackmailed him into having sex regularly until Ron's family moved out of town. As a grown up, Ron had a history of depression, road rage, and getting into fights. We worked on safe space imagery for Ron and for parts who held the violence and depression. Initial strategies included the violent parts agreeing to sit in the back seat of the car doing safe space imagery while Ron did the driving. Then we began working on the past trauma. A manager part blocked all access to exiles. I told the blocker part that we would not work with any exiles until the blocker agreed. Ron was curious about the blocker and found out the blocker thought Ron would become violent or fall apart if he allowed Ron to connect with exiles. I asked Ron how old the blocker thought he was, and the blocker said 9. Ron asked the blocker to look at him while Ron looked back at him and let the blocker know how old he was and that he had lots of strengths that he didn't have when he was 9. The blocker was impressed, but still had concerns. I suggested Ron ask the blocker if he would be willing to allow Ron five % access to one of the exiles. The blocker agreed. Ron then felt some connection to the exile and was able to witness and unburden some of what the exile was holding. The exile felt stronger, and the blocker felt like his job had gotten easier.

Complications

The most difficult treatment processes I have had have been working together with clients who have been through inadequate to incompetent prior treatment. When coping skill development has been neglected and/or there have been major boundary violations (unintentional by therapists who encourage dependency by over providing comfort or working too hard, or intentional by therapists who prey on vulnerable clients), and dissociative boundaries have been eroded, the treatment process is much more complicated. In these cases, I work on building in coping and management skills and do the best I can to give the client control during the witnessing process. Repair can take a long time and the treatment process remains more difficult than it would have been.

Example: One woman was able to put some of her complex system in safe spaces and use containers during trauma processing, but her ability was limited. Once we chose a target to work on, we were in it for the duration. This often meant several weeks of hell for her consisting of increased self-destructive behaviors, drinking, sleeping excessively, inability to function, etc. And then we would get through it, and she would make progress. was lucky to have the resources not to have to work.

For a while, we would have some comparatively peaceful sessions and then she would come in looking like she had never made any progress. At first, I would panic, thinking something had gone wrong, but later realized that it was really a pattern of progress, which I coined a *"crisis of progress."* For some dissociative clients progress is made and then a part or group of parts decide *"Ok it's our turn now, she looks like she has a good enough therapist!"* and pop out. Or it may be that the unconscious says, *"She's stronger now, she can handle this traumatic material which is even more difficult."* In these confusing times, I have gotten used to asking, *"Is there someone new present? Check inside."* Of course, it is not a totally new part, just a part or parts that have been more deeply dissociated and have now surfaced. These parts often are very disoriented, and do not have coping skills, or do not have fully operational coping skills.

When a part pops out, looks panicked and says, *"Who are you and how did I get here?"* I explain, *"I am Joanne, I work with people who had difficult childhoods and help them feel better. Do you know (name of client)? She brought you here and we have been working together to make things better."* I invite the client to join us in this process which assists with the development of internal communication and cooperation. I say, *"(Name of client) tell this part how you got to know me and what we have been working on together."* Sometimes this process is easy, and sometimes it is not, but the process of getting this part or new layer of parts oriented to treatment and the present goes faster because of prior progress. There may not seem to be any connection among dissociated parts but there is always some.

The Later Stage of Phase 2: Reconfiguring and Grieving

Clinicians will notice that as traumatic material is resolved, dissociative barriers dissolve and the system of parts becomes reconfigured. Reconfiguring can take many different shapes. One client had a group of deaf parts who were suddenly able to hear once we finished processing the reasons for needing deaf parts. Another client suddenly saw colours in more depth.

Grieving is an important part of healing and, can be confused with depression. It may be important to reassure clients and parts of clients that the grief and sadness they are feeling is normal and not a sign that they are falling into depression. People need to grieve what happened, and all the time they spent in life before they could heal. This includes time spent in therapies that did not lead to healing or made things worse.

Integration of Parts

As mentioned before, integration can be thought of narrowly as in many parts integrating into one, or more broadly as integration into a non-trauma based Self-led system. It is important to realize and respect that many people with dissociative disorders have healed comprehensively in therapies where the goal has been integration. Do people ever integrate into one or does everyone continue to have ego states with or without the concept of Self? Perhaps it is similar to gender identity, which was once thought of more rigidly as strictly male or female but is now believed to be more fluid. This is how I view trauma treatment—fluid with the client taking the lead in whatever works best for him/her. Personally, I think people integrate into a healthy Self-led system if treatment is done right.

Life Review

How do you know when the trauma work is done? Sometimes it is evident and sometimes it isn't. One client bought us happy integration t-shirts, only to have a more deeply dissociated group of parts pop out and wreak havoc. This persisted until they were witnessed and unburdened. Sometimes there is a sense that something is missing and needs attention. In these cases, I have the client do a life review - a fast-forward visualization from what they know of their mother's pregnancy with them to the present. The instruction is, *"If something positive comes up, to stay there and let the positive feelings/experience/relationship soak in deeply. If something negative comes up, let me know and so we can witness and unburden it."*

Example: A client remembered experiences of being loved by her grandmother when she was four. She let these positive feelings soak in. Her grandmother died soon after that. As she progressed through the life review, she remembered a time when her third-grade teacher made fun of her for wearing a dirty coat to school when it was hot out. She had worn the coat to hide ligature marks on her wrists caused when her father and some of his friends had tied her up and abused her. This school incident and others had been obscured by more violent traumas.

Summary

This chapter has presented options for titrating and organizing traumatic material, so the witnessing remains in control and productive. Some clients will need to use all the recommended coping skills and controls (containers, safe spaces, TV with the PIP, etc), and some less. Some parts and or/traumatic events will require all the controls even if other parts in their system have needed less. I try to remember that the client managed to live through these traumas as a child, so no matter how difficult or hopeless it can feel, we can work through them together.

CHAPTER 13

Phase 3: Integrated Functioning: Adjusting to a Life Not Organized by Trauma

Introduction:

The client enters Phase 3 when they are done with Phase 2. In this phase of treatment, clients spend time adjusting to a life not controlled by the burdens of the past, adjusting to not being dissociative, and continue adjusting to a more Self-led life. Treatment sessions look more like traditional IFS sessions, although it is important for clinicians to remember that it is still possible for dissociative material or untreated groups of parts to surface, necessitating a return to Phase 2, or perhaps even to Phase 1. This can be disconcerting for both clients and therapists, but it is a normal part of healing. I sometimes say, *"This healing business can be like debugging a computer. You have to use it to figure out where the bugs are, and every time we find one and deal with it, it is one less thing to cause problems later."*

> **Note:** It is simply a fact that there are clients who cannot make it to Phase 3. Some may not be able to sufficiently work through Phase 2 as their lives may be too chaotic or they may be too fragile by virtue of age or physical illness. I continue to hold out the possibility of healing and use clinical judgement.

Phase 3: Integrated Functioning: Adjusting to a Life Not Organized by Trauma

Often, clients must spend time continuing the grieving they began in Phase 2 of all the losses of time and life experiences they missed during their childhoods and adulthoods. Most will have at the very least, underperformed at work or spent time in dysfunctional relationships, and are now at a point in their lives where they can look back and see how different their life *could* have been had they grown up with healthier parents. Along with grieving, the focus in this phase is on the client dealing with whatever else needs to be done for healing. Some of what may need to be dealt with are changes in relationships as a result of healing. Some need to go into couples therapy to process these changes and some divorce, as once they heal, they are often able to more realistically evaluate their spouse. Other issues that may need to be dealt with include work, changes in relationship toward one's family of origin, and existential and spiritual concerns. Some people will need to work on coping skills to deal with normal life—or what passes for 'normal.' One of my clients joined a book group with 'normal' people and was aghast at everything they avoided. She said one woman never drove over bridges, and another could not talk with a friend about a disagreement. I sometimes think people who are forced to work on themselves become healthier than "normal" people.

Another important part of Phase 3 is psychoeducation. Along with specific needs of clients, I routinely cover stress management and the knowledge that under stress we all tend to go back to early ways of coping. This means these clients may find themselves dissociating or becoming blended with parts when stressed. This needs to be normalized so it can be dealt with without shame or feeling like a failure, and I always give reminders that the fire drill is useful even when therapy is over.

Ending Treatment

Eventually, the client and therapist will look back on the whole treatment and begin the process of termination. This process will need to be tailored to fit the needs and dynamics of the individual client. It is a time for careful reflection and review as the work of healing has been immense. One client said, *"No one knows the 'me' who first came to see you, or what we went through in this healing. They know me now and would never guess what I've gone through."* The relationship of the client and therapist has been extremely important and pivotal, and it will remain so. I tend to space out a client's sessions until they are no longer needed regularly and maintain an open-door policy for clients to come back for "tune-ups" if needed. Many clients have kept in touch with me by sending cards periodically or have emailed just to let me know how they are doing.

My work in treating people who have had these extremely difficult childhoods has taught me a lot about the horrors that some adults and older children inflict on younger children. It has also humbled me as I have worked with these individuals and witnessed first-hand, the enormous amount of healing that has occurred. Being part of the solution to child abuse and neglect has been a gift.

CHAPTER 14

Terminations Due to the Therapist's Needs

Introduction

There are times when treatment needs to end after a few sessions, months, or years. There are concrete reasons e.g., when a therapist is moving away, becomes very ill, or is retiring. Then there are more complex reasons, one of which may be therapist countertransference, client transference issues, professional judgement, and/or the therapist's range of knowledge and competence. No therapist can work with everyone. In this chapter, we will discuss communicating the need to end treatment with a client and planned versus unplanned terminations.

The General Process

Before beginning discussion with a client about the need to terminate, make sure you have dealt with any issues and feelings you have in either consultation or your own therapy. Once you have developed a plan and are ready to meet with your client, use the fire drill to prepare for the session by dealing with any last-minute issues, feelings, and concerns your parts might have. It is extremely important to have enough Self energy before beginning these difficult and often painful sessions.

It is normal to have feelings with the client. For instance, one therapist told me, she and her client both had tears in their eyes. Another therapist told a client, *"I don't want this to be happening. Right now, I feel totally numb about it. I think I'm feeling anger and sadness inside."* Clients whose childhoods necessitated hypervigilance, will pick up on your feelings anyway. Expressing these emotions normalizes and clarifies their own responses.

Give clients whatever notice makes sense and is possible, so there is ideally enough time to discuss the need to end treatment, tie up necessary treatment issues, and transition the client to a new therapist. Or acknowledge that you are not able to give them enough notice and apologize. Be as honest as you can, without disclosing so much that you overly burden the client or make yourself too vulnerable.

> Note: Sometimes this process flows without difficulty. Usually this is when the decision is reached in session mutually.

Planned vs Unplanned Terminations

A planned termination happens when you need to end treatment and you have some time to process the ending with the client. This could happen if you get a new job, or you need to move out of town. It could also happen if you decide to close your practice or retire, or you may be diagnosed with an illness that requires you to be out of work for a long period of time. Being honest with the client is the best policy while ensuring that there is enough time for a thoughtful process. If you do not have enough time, plan as thoughtful a process as is possible.

An unplanned termination happens when there is an emergency over which you have no control and there is no time to process the termination. It is important to remember that C-PTSD and DD clients often have histories of abandonment, betrayal, and attachment issues. They may also have a history of inappropriate and badly handled terminations from previous therapists. Thus, the better you handle the termination process, the easier and more efficient it will be for the client and their next therapist.

In addition, a well-done, respectful termination process can help the client work through some of the painful issues from the past. For example, one client was eventually able to reflect that her previous therapist had been honest around ending their therapy relationship even though it felt awful at the time. Another client contrasted her father's abandonment of his family and her expectation of future abandonment with how her therapist was managing their termination process.

This does not mean it will be a smooth or easy process, but our job is to ensure we do our part of the process as well as we can. Clients can have an extremely difficult time with the ending of treatment and even when we do try our very best, that may at times be unavoidable.

Planned and Uncomplicated Terminations

It is important to be clear about the need for the termination and to take responsibility for it.

Example: *"My spouse's job was just transferred to Ohio. After giving this much thought, I've decided to close my practice in four months. I'm sorry I couldn't give you more notice. I really want to hear all your questions about this and for us to work out what's best for you."*

Example: *"I'm planning on retiring in two years. I'm letting you know now as this will give us time to finish some of the work we've been doing. It will also give us time to think about what you want to do about therapy after I retire."*

Example: *"I don't want to complicate your life and the work we've been doing, but I need to tell you I was just diagnosed with cancer and will need to take extended time off. My doctor says the treatment will be extensive and has recommended I close my practice with the hope of opening it again in the future."* Or: *"I've just been diagnosed with terminal cancer and can't keep working. We will only have two more sessions to talk about it. I'm really sorry about this and I'm feeling sad."*

Make sure you take responsibility for any promises you have made and apologize for not being able to keep them. If you think you might have made a promise but cannot remember it, ask the client. These clients remember promises and a broken promise will often be a sign for parts that the present is just like the past. This will inadvertently reinforce their belief that no one, especially therapists, are to be trusted in any way and could subsequently complicate future treatment. It is also recommended that you apologize for implied promises.

Example: *"When we started working together, I thought I'd be working for a long time. I know I promised you that we'd work together until you healed. I am so sorry I can't keep my promise."*

Explore the termination with all parts. Do not allow the client to deflect the importance of this stage of treatment. Some trauma clients are very good at deflecting and to protect themselves or the therapist, may avoid talking about any painful and difficult feelings they may have including anger, shame, and betrayal. Initiating a discussion around ending treatment can be very difficult for the therapist, and deflections may feel like a relief, but it's a mistake to use a client's avoidance to make things easier. A client might say any of the following when they are feeling the opposite: *"People always leave me, I'm used to it,"* or *"I'll be fine, you'll find me a good therapist,"* or *"I don't want to waste time talking about it, let's keep doing therapy on my stuff until you leave,"* or *"You've been a great therapist, and I've learned so much from you and grown so much. Don't worry about it at all; I'll be fine."*

> Note: A client told me 'fine' means:
>
> - Fucked up,
> - Insecure,
> - Neurotic, and
> - Emotional.

One word of caution: Deal with your feelings regarding the termination (i.e., guilt, shame, etc.) in your own treatment or in consultation. Some therapists go into high gear and try and finish as much work with the client as possible. This has the risk of pushing the client past their ability to make progress or to inadvertently make the next therapist look substandard.

Discuss what you've learned from the client and what you will miss. Talk about your sense of loss if that is appropriate.

Sudden Unplanned Termination

Things happen. Circumstances determine how difficult this will be for the client, and prior planning by the therapist can be a big help. Here are some examples of sudden, unplanned terminations:

- The therapist becomes severely injured, disabled, or dies in an accident or of a sudden physical event like a stroke, aneurism, etc.
- The therapist or a family member is murdered or commits suicide.
- Anything happens that means you can no longer deal with the complexity of notifying clients.

Example: A client came into treatment for complex PTSD. It was soon clear she had DID. The therapist had the skills but then her father was diagnosed with terminal cancer. She realized she did not have the emotional energy to continue with the client.

> **Note:** Therapists may discover that a client in their practice has a dissociative disorder. When this happens, they can often learn what is necessary to competently treat their client. This necessitates having the time needed and motivation to learn. It is important to realize that many therapists began treating people with dissociative disorders this way and there is no shame in doing so. See the appendix for additional information.

Deciding you don't have the time or interest is not a problem. We all have different areas of expertise and interest; we all have different life circumstances that allow us to have more or less time to learn something new.

Example: A therapist was diagnosed with a terminal illness. The therapist told each of her clients some version of: "*The last thing I want to do is complicate your life, but I need to tell you, I've been diagnosed with cancer and will need to close my practice, so I'll be working with you to find you another therapist to transfer you to.*" Then the therapist answered questions, based on how much information each client wanted. The therapist had also decided what information she was comfortable with and was appropriate to share. Her bottom-line answer was: "*I have pancreatic cancer, it's terminal, and I'll be spending the time I have getting the treatment I need to have the best life possible with what time I've got left.*"

Professional Wills

What would happen to your practice and clients if you suddenly had to stop working immediately or died? Does a colleague have a current list of your clients, consultees, and their contact information? Is there a plan for what happens to your records? If you do not have this figured out already, you should consider planning for the future by preparing a professional will.

All therapists need to have a professional will. A therapist's professional will is an agreement with one or more therapists for what happens if you are suddenly unable to return to work. It is important to discuss this with whomever you are appointing as executor, and it is important to draft this will in accordance with the ethics and regulations of the relevant profession. For instance, one regulation for social workers in Massachusetts is that their spouses cannot be appointed as executor. Many therapy associations have templates available.

Key items in a professional will include:

- Who will notify clients of what happened?
- Who will take care of referring clients to new therapists?
- Who will take custody of records and destroy them in a timely manner?
- Who will shut down the therapist's office and/or business?
- Setting up a stipend to defray the expenses for the person who will take care of these things, which realistically can take hours of work.

Anyone who has had to step in to close the practice of someone who has suddenly died knows how important professional wills are personally, professionally, and for clients. Having a professional will, taking the time to terminate properly and apologizing for circumstances and any broken promises will eventually be healing for our clients and help them in the process of moving on.

Complex Terminations

Some clients threaten to file lawsuits or board complaints. When this happens, it gives you the chance to ask parts of the system why this feels necessary. Sometimes it will be because the client is angry or there is a painful treatment issue they want to avoid. In this case, it may be possible to process the issue and continue treatment. On the other hand, there are clients who have parts who are psychopathic and dangerous or are introjects of psychopathic or dangerous abusers. There are also clients who want revenge for one reason or another. In general, a client filing is a boundary violation, and the therapy relationship needs to end. One of the prerequisites for doing therapy is that the therapist needs to feel safe (or safe enough) while working with someone, and it is difficult to feel safe with a client who threatens to or does file a board complaint or lawsuit.

If this happens, consult a lawyer who is aware of your professional association and its guidelines and plan a termination with the client that is legally defensible. If it is necessary to provide referrals, one recommendation is to supply names of local agencies who have legal services available to their employees. This is generally not something to deal with in private practice. Some clients may say: "*But all of us except that one part want to keep working with you.*" or, "*That part didn't mean it, and we can work it through.*" Maybe, but the risk factor may be too great, unless you are working in an environment (like a prison) where this behavior is expected and manageable.

It is also often important to notify your malpractice association if you think there's a possibility of someone filing against you.

> "There are two kinds of therapists, ones who've had a lawsuit or board complaint filed and ones who will. We work with people who are sometimes very troubled and/or have family members who are sometimes very troubled."—Stephan Frankel, PHD, LD (via personal communication)

In the case of a client or a former client filing a legitimate board complaint or one the board sees as legitimate; you may get sanctioned. This means you may be ordered to close your practice for a period of time or even permanently. Follow the advice of your lawyer. I know therapists who made mistakes, had board complaints filed against them, got whatever education and consultation the board required, and fulfilled all requirements while growing through the process, and are again practicing therapists. As difficult as this is, working with your parts, taking things one step at a time, and growing through the process is the way to go.

If you are ordered to close your practice for a length of time, it can be extremely helpful to work with a therapist or consultant on your feelings about it so you can have as much access to Self energy as possible when discussing it with clients. One way of broaching the conversation with clients in preparation for the required time off is to say: *"I'm sorry I need to complicate things, but I'm needing to close my practice for X length of time."*

Again, being honest is important, and you may need to say something about the circumstances, e.g., *"There was a board complaint filed against me and the board found against me."* Again, consult with a lawyer on what you can say and what needs to remain confidential. Clients need enough information to make your absence comprehensible without being overwhelmed and burdened.

Complicated Countertransference and Transference Issues

No one can work with everyone. Even therapists with extensive experience and skills can find themselves needing to terminate with a client. For example, a therapist may be deeply involved in working with a client and unexpectedly discover some unworked through trauma and attachment wounds of their own. Sometimes these things can be worked through and the treatment can continue, and sometimes it is best to refer the client. Part of being a competent and ethical therapist is being able to identify when a client needs to be transferred. Humility is an important attribute to being a good therapist.

> Note: Steven Frankel, PhD. JD. ABPP. wrote, "If we're going to ask our patients to go to their deepest and darkest places, we need to be willing to go to our own deepest and darkest places."

If a client is getting worse or is not making progress and nothing you are doing shifts this circumstance, they need to be referred. If a client is excessively demanding, is draining your energy, and you cannot manage it anymore, you need to prioritize your own needs. Aside from the obvious need for self-care, another important reason is that if one client is demanding a huge amount of your energy, your other clients will eventually suffer from lack of attention on your part.

Some clients are experts at identifying therapists' vulnerabilities and on using them to deskill the therapist. Whether this can be worked out depends on the therapist's ability to work on her/his issues, and on the client. One of my clients told me, *"My superpower was eviscerating female therapists."* She came by this ability naturally, as the power in her family had been held by her sadistic mother. After suffering through a reenactment full of pain, shame, rage, and sadness, we managed to work it through. She is now finished with treatment and living a different life. If I could do it over, I would get more consultation and go back into my own therapy sooner.

> Note: There are therapists who should not be therapists due to being sexual predators, being incompetent, and/or having too many problems of their own. They have the capacity to inflict tremendous damage on all including these vulnerable clients.

Example: A professional woman came into treatment because of depression and being marginalized at work and in her life in general. She appeared eager to start treatment and capable of healing. After several months where the therapy remained stagnant and the client not helped enough, the therapist, who had considerable skill, realized she needed to transfer the client. Her best guess about why the client wasn't making progress was that the client's issues somehow mirrored some unresolved preverbal issues of her own which she was not aware of.

At this point the therapist had two choices: One, get back into her own therapy and resolve her issues, which would be good for the therapist and could lead to resolving the stuck place and, two, refer the client to another therapist. In this case, the therapist decided the countertransference/transference issues were too complex to continue with the client. She discussed her realization that the treatment was not working and indicated that it was best that they found another therapist for the client. The client asked, *"Is it me?"* And the therapist said, *"No, I think it's me. I think some of my issues are too similar to yours, and it's just not working. You deserve to heal."* The client was referred to another therapist and began to make progress.

Example. The client was diagnosed with DID. The therapist, wanting to be helpful but not understanding the boundaries and complexities in working with someone with DID, was willing to exchange multiple emails and have phone call contact between sessions. The client began writing longer and longer emails more frequently and making excessive phone calls and texts in between sessions. The therapist was burning out, her family life was suffering, and she was considering getting another job.

In consultation, the therapist realized she did not have the necessary skills to treat this client, located a therapist who could, and transferred the client. She also got back into therapy to deal with her own trauma history and got more training.

Example: A woman came into treatment to work on work problems. After a few sessions, it was clear the "work problems" were the result of untreated DID. Additionally, the therapist, who specialized in work problems did not have the training necessary to help her. She appropriately asked a colleague who was a trauma therapist, to take on the case. During the transition, the new therapist taught the client system-wide coping skills and the client began to stabilize. At this point, the original therapist decided to keep the client, and not refer her as originally planned. Now back with the original therapist, the client once again became destabilized. At this point, the therapist wanted to refer her again and a confusing time ensued with more back and forth between the two therapists. The original therapist eventually felt that her client was being "stolen" by the trauma therapist because the client was paying her full fee. She pulled on the client's dependency and abandonment issues until sadly, the client decided to stay with her and discontinue treatment with the trauma therapist, with whom she had been making tremendous progress.

20 years later, the therapist referred the client to a different therapist for consultation because of the client's extreme dependency, abandonment issues, and dissociative symptoms. By coincidence, that consultant, concerned about the woman's lack of progress in her years of treatment, randomly asked the former consultant/therapist for a consult.

This is a very sad cautionary tale. It's a travesty that this client who had the capacity to heal got trapped in a treatment with a therapist whose issues clouded her personal judgement and resulted in her being paid for 20 years more for inadequate treatment. This negligence on the part of the therapist doomed the client to years, and maybe a lifetime of additional pain and impaired functioning.

Summary

Therapists often feel horrible when having to terminate with a client whether it is planned or unplanned. These are normal situations, however, and have to be dealt with. Our clients were brought up in families filled with faulty mirroring, attachment problems, betrayals, bad boundaries, and confusion. It is important that we are honest, straightforward, and human. How we terminate with someone, however difficult it is, can be healing if it is done honestly, directly, and respectfully. It is also important for all of us to have Professional Wills in place to manage unexpected, unplanned circumstances.

CHAPTER 15
Advanced Considerations

Introduction

This chapter provides information on advanced considerations including:

- Therapist Stance for Treatment of Dissociative Disorders
- Treatment Trajectories
- Countertransference and Projective Identification
- Reenactments and Enactments
- The Karpman Drama Triangle
- Five Transference and Countertransference Patterns,
- Assessing Potential for Violence
- How Offenders Influence their Victim's Perceptions
- The BITE Model of Destructive Mind Control
- Client Suicide
- The Compass of Shame

Therapist Stance for Treatment of Dissociative Disorders

- Check for Self energy before sessions and periodically during sessions.
- Do not expect or try to stay rigidly in Self. It is necessary to create space for nonverbal communications by allowing ourselves to slide out of Self and experience projective identifications, countertransferences, and reenactments.
  - *"For the deepest growth to take place, patients needed to allow themselves to be a 'mess' within our relationship, and in order for me to truly know them, I had to become a part of the mess in a way that I could experience internally."* (Chefetz and Bromberg 2004)
  - The fire drill is one way to get out of the 'mess' and back into Self. Through this process, nonverbal communication can begin to be translated into words.
- Adjust expectations according to ability of the client. (See Treatment Trajectory section below.)
- Try to be nondefensive with criticism and apologize as needed. Porges PhD, a neuroscientist recommends that if you want people to be open and engaged, communicate acceptance.
- Your voice needs to generally be modulated, relaxed, nonjudgemental, and curious. It is also important to be real and have a range of feelings.
- If you are working harder than the client, there is something wrong
- Do not become attached to the outcome. We do not have that much control.
- Be attached to providing competent treatment and doing the best you can.

- Have and project gentle confidence and the belief that healing is and will be happening.
- Sometimes, you need to take a stand. If you know your client is doing something that could put themselves or their children in physical or legal danger, take a stand. No one took a stand when these clients were children.
- Teach, model, and have good self-care.

And these last two points which come from the book *Treating Trauma-Related Dissociation* (Steele et al. 2016), a book filled with wisdom and a must-have if you are treating dissociative disordered clients:

- Identify your primary attachment style and that of your client's. Your attachment style may have an impact on how you work with your client. For example, if you and your client both have avoidant attachment styles, you may unconsciously play that out in therapy.
- Know the signs of being over or under involved with clients.

Treatment Trajectories

It is extremely helpful to know what treatment trajectory your client falls into. Around 2011, during an International Society for the Study of Trauma and Dissociation annual conference, Richard Kluft, MD gave a lecture on characteristics of clients with fast, medium, and slow treatment trajectories based on his many years of providing therapy and consultation. At that time, I was treating and stressing out about a woman with a very complex abuse history who was making glacially slow progress. I kept trying to figure out what I was doing wrong and what I could be doing better. It just seemed that nothing was working to make her healing go any faster. Kluft's lecture was a relief and gave me a template for understanding why some clients' progress faster than others.

Why do clients have different treatment trajectories? Sometimes it is because of temperament and sometimes the circumstances of their childhoods, including the type of abuse they suffered, the number of perpetrators, frequent family moves disrupting community relationships that could have been supportive, or the presence of someone who actually or appeared to care. See examples below. Sometimes, it is because of circumstances like war and poverty, or inadequate and damaging prior treatment.

Example: As a young child, a woman had been sent a postcard by her aunts. She believed that if they knew what was going on in her family, they would rescue her. In her 30s she found out that they had known. Her belief had given her important hope throughout her childhood.

Example: A woman carried her grandmothers love in her heart and knew her grandmother had protected her. Her grandmother died when she was 4.

Clients can also change their treatment trajectories. Kluft spoke of a client who went from slow to medium after eighteen years of treatment. I have also had similar experiences with clients.

This section is based on my notes from Kluft's lecture. (Please note: No one has all of the characteristics listed in these categories!)

Fast Trajectory Clients:

- Tend to have an easier time developing a good therapeutic relationship.
- Are individuated from their family of origin.
- Have the ability to tolerate pain and are not avoidant.
- They like you and like coming for therapy, but they want to heal and be done.

- They are active learners and work on things during the week.
- They have supportive relationships.

Medium Trajectory Clients:

- Tend to have more depression.
- Their relationships tend to be more problematic.
- Are more passive and prefer to call you than use coping skills.
- Tend to ruminate more about their memories, wondering if they really happened or not.
- Are the most active readers of books about dissociation and treatment.

Slow Trajectory Clients:

- Experience more complex patterns of borderline personality disorder and tend to have more incidences of severe major depression and chronic pain.
- Experience more trance logic, fantasy proneness, suggestibility, and denial.
- Are more enmeshed with their family of origin and try harder to forgive abusers. They are more often re-victimized.
- Make more allegations of witnessing violent deaths and ritual abuse.
- Show severe narcissistic vulnerability and characterological passivity.
- Express less to no overt anger, tend to be phobic of pain, and are avoidant.
- Their response to medications tends to be worse, and they have more side effects.

- They have severe attachment issues.
- They attempt to remake the world to suit them.

Countertransference and Projective Identification

Dalenberg (2000) wrote, "*Traumatized patients often have lived daily with the experience of having physical and emotional reality denied and distorted...The therapist who is unwilling to own countertransference feelings is less able to help the client learn to have faith in his or her own emotional perception—when it is accurate- or to differentiate projected from actual emotional experiences.*" This is particularly important for dissociative patients who will pick up on whatever vulnerabilities we have and need to have their awarenesses validated. It is a more vulnerable, present place to work from, and enables the client to figure out how to make accurate judgments of people, after living through childhoods filled with faulty mirroring and parental denial.

Example: I did not want to meet with a client who was not making enough progress. I found him tedious and could think of lots of other things I'd rather do. In thinking about him, and while getting in Self in preparation for the session, I realized I felt like we were missing something. I said to him, *"I've been thinking about you and our work together. I'm thinking we're missing something. You aren't making the progress I think you should be making. What do you think?"* He said, *"I do too."* This led us to uncover a layer of abuse he had not consciously been aware of, felt enormous shame about and was avoiding.

Example: I felt confused, hopeless, and had no idea how to help a client make progress. I said, *"I have no idea what to do right now. I feel confused, hopeless, and stuck, and I'm wondering if this is how you felt as a kid.... We've been here before, and I know if we keep struggling together we'll figure it out and make progress through this."*

I had gotten lost in the feelings. Then, I realized that although I truly was not sure what to do next, that I was also picking up on my client's nonverbal communication of having me *feel* what her childhood was like. I put that into words and then she could also acknowledge it in words. Finally, I reflected on our past experiences in therapy and reminded her of them. The combination of hopelessness and dissociation can make it difficult for our clients to track progress.

Projective Identification

Projective Identification is an unconscious defense in which a person with qualities and/or feelings that they want to avoid or do not want to have, project these qualities/feelings onto another. The recipient of these projections, influenced by the authority of the other (as in a parent projecting onto a child) or who has a resonance with the projection (as in a client projecting feeling hopelessness onto a therapist) takes in the projection and identifies it as their own.

Example: A therapist experienced strong feelings of incompetence while meeting with a client. Initially, the therapist thought, *"Why did I pick up this client? I don't know enough to treat her."* Then, the therapist realized that even though the client was difficult, she/he had made progress and that the therapist was picking up the client's projections. This was eventually confirmed. The therapist, having her own feelings of incompetence, was particularly receptive to picking up these feelings. Specifically, the therapist used the fire drill to identify an exile who carried the belief that she was not good enough.

Example: During a session, I felt angry in relation to a client who was looking calm. I said, *"It feels like there's some anger floating around in the room. Is anyone inside you feeling anger about anything?"* At first, she said, "No," then after a few minutes said, *"I feel it now."*

Example: For several sessions, I felt exhausted when meeting with one client. I missed it at first because I had not been sleeping well. Then came a session after a night when I had slept well, and I asked her, *"What is going on inside you? I'm just wondering because I actually slept well last night and was feeling alert, but now I'm suddenly exhausted. Is there a part who wants me to go to sleep?"* She acknowledged that there was a part who wanted to avoid our session. In following sessions, whenever I felt sleepy, I'd ask if that part was present. She generally was and that enabled us to acknowledge that there was something difficult the part wanted to avoid. We then had to figure out how to talk about it.

Example: I was talking to a client on the phone about rescheduling a session when I suddenly had an image of violently slapping her across the face. At the next session I said, *"The weirdest thing happened to me. You know I care about you and would never hurt you, but when we were talking on the phone, I had the image of slapping you across the face."* The client immediately switched into a part who said, *"Slap me, rape me, throw me against the wall, I like to be hurt. It's why I was born."* Because the client could not avoid being abused as a child, she had a part who welcomed it and easily lubricated when she was going to be raped.

Reenactments

Reenactments occur in therapy when *"...patient and therapist become the inevitable participants in transference enactment, each unwittingly playing a role written from the patient's past. By creatively welcoming inevitable enactment, the therapist and patient can work through otherwise uninterpretable material."* [i.e., nonverbal]. (Baker 1998). More simply said, it's when the therapist's issues react with the client's and they get played out in treatment.

Our job is to pull ourselves out of the unconscious reenactment and get it into words. Van der Kolk (1989) said, *"Reactivation of past learning is relatively automatic: contextual stimuli directly evoke stored memories without conscious awareness of the transition. The more similar the contextual stimuli are to conditions prevailing at the time of the original storage of memories, the more likely the probability of retrieval.*" So, if circumstances are right, we slide into reenactments. Checking for Self periodically will help identify them sooner rather than later.

Example: One client's abusive and extremely complicated mother was externally very different from my mother. After the client and I spent too long in a painful reenactment in which we passed back and forth victim and perpetrator roles, we figured out what set it off and then eventually figured out that under the surface, our mothers had some strikingly similar characteristics. I got back in treatment to work on the issues it brought up for me, apologized to the client, and took responsibility for my part. Treatment got back on track. These "bad weeks" as we referred to them, were something we returned to over and over at different points in treatment as different parts needed to work through their issues about them.

Example: A client and I got into a pattern where during sessions I would lose it and become overtly angry at her. As we discussed the pattern, the client said, *"I know why this is happening! I had no impact on my father or my old therapist, who, no matter what I did or said stayed 'understanding and kind.' It is such a relief that I can have an impact on you!"* (Note: Her previous therapist had bad boundaries, was very destructive and eventually lost his license.) It was interesting that I had felt bad and less than competent because I had been getting overtly angry at her, but then it turned out that my becoming overtly angry was what she needed!

Advanced Considerations

The Karpman Drama Triangle

Karpman developed the Drama Triangle in 1968 to explain relationships in families where there are alcoholic family members. Turkus and Kahler (2006) added the "non rescuer" to the rescuer pole as in most families where there is abuse, there is no rescuer. I added "persecutor" to this pole as in some families there are 2 persecutors and no rescuer or bystander. These patterns of relationships are another useful way to track and discuss nonverbal communication, countertransference and enactments. Therefore, tune into how you feel as you meet with clients. As Richard Schwartz stated, *"Self pulls for Self"* if your client is in a victim position, this will pull for you being in either persecutor mode or rescuer mode. If you are working from a rescuer mode your client will be pulled into the victim role. Noticing these dynamics and discussing them leads to awareness and change.

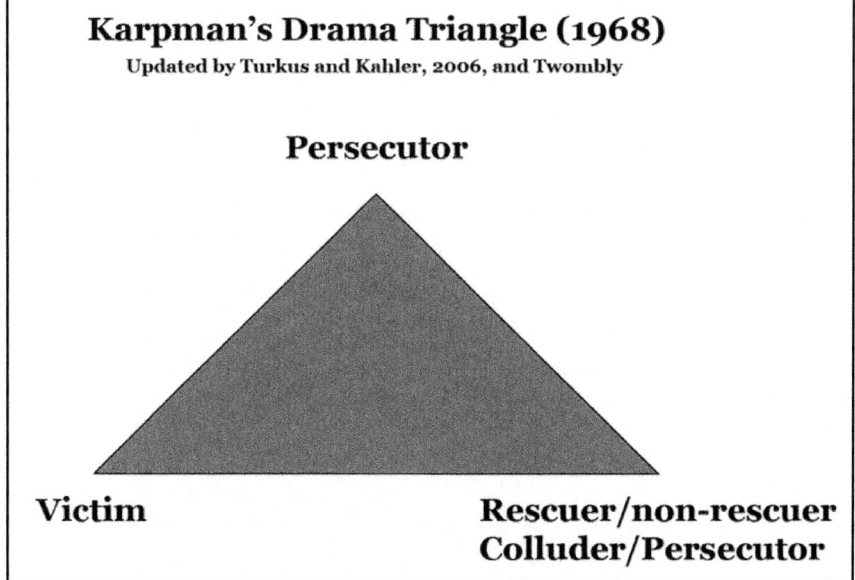

Example: A long-term client was unable to answer a question in spite of all the work we had done together. I encouraged her to speak and then went on to make a few comments like, "*Oh, come on, we've worked together for ages, you can tell me!*" She got quieter and quieter. By the next session, I had identified that I had begun badgering her (persecutor role) while she got more and more silent (victim role). She agreed about this insight, and we made progress identifying when she was in victim role and I in persecutor role.

Example: A therapist often spoke to a client in between sessions for extensive periods of time. Using the fire drill, we identified (in consultation) a part of her who was locked into rescuer mode. This part had been inadvertently supporting the client in victim mode.

Example: A client's spouse periodically berated her. We identified that this happened when she was in the victim role. We worked on her being able to ground herself, also known as getting into Self or into a part with more Self energy, and when she was able to do that, the berating stopped.

Example: A client with C-PTSD exclaimed, "*I must have the word 'victim' tattooed to my forehead!*" We identified that she was taught to be (and indeed was) in the victim role as a child and had continued that role. This meant she was bullied by anyone so inclined.

When working with the client's internal system of parts, watch for parts who internally play out these roles. There will be victim parts, rescuer/non rescuer/bystander parts and persecutor parts interacting with each other. This is similar to polarization.

> Note: Read *"The Power of Ted*"* by David Emerald (2009). It is an excellent Self Help book that has helped many people with interpersonal dynamics. The core of the book shows how to track and make use of the Karpman Drama Triangle and discusses its resolution.

Five Transference and Countertransference Patterns (Davies and Frawley, 1994, 1999)

Sometimes these patterns are easy to identify and sometimes they can be more subtle. Knowing and being aware of them helps identify protective parts, managers, and exiles within the client, and within countertransference/transference reactions in the therapy relationship. The sooner these patterns can be identified, the sooner they can be addressed. This decreases the risk of acting on them or having them complicate the treatment.

- The Unseeing, Uninvolved Parent and the Unseen, Neglected Child
- The Sadistic Abuser and the Helpless, Impotently Enraged Victim
- The Seducer and the Seduced
- The Idealized, Omnipotent Rescuer and the Entitled Child, and
- The Certain Believer and the Chronic Doubter

Assess Potential for Violence When Necessary

I know one therapist who was killed by a client during a psychotic episode that was fueled by trauma. These 4 elements are listed in Gavin De Becker's 1998 book: *The Gift of Fear*. Use them to evaluate and consider the possibility of threats to your own safety. If you perceive any potential threats of violence, take steps to minimize them in whatever way you need to.

The 4 Elements

1. Perceived Justification: does the person think violence is justified?

2. Perceived Alternatives: are there perceived alternatives to violence?
3. Perceived Consequences: is the consequence favourable or tolerable?
4. Perceived Ability: can they?

How Offenders Influence their Victim's Perceptions (Salter, 1995)

- Gas lighting.
- Pretending everything is normal.
- Denying harming the victim.
- Uses victim's sexual response against the victim.
- Using dependency/attachment needs against the victim.
- Confusion techniques.
- Continue family life as if nothing happened.
- Not abusing siblings (or lying).
- Being totally different in life outside the family or when others are present.
- Raping them at night, then sending them to Catholic confession where sexual contact is a mortal sin.

The BITE Model of Destructive Mind Control

Some of our complex trauma clients will have been brought up in destructive cults or have been entrapped and abused in them outside of their families. Additionally, some families function very similarly to cults. The BITE model (Hassen, 2000) helps identify dynamics in cults and these families. Further information can be found on Hassen's web sites: https://Freedomofmind.com and https://BITEModeAnalysis.wordpress.com

BITE: Promote dependency and obedience by:

- Behavior Control
- Information Control
- Thought Control
- Emotional Control

Client Suicide

Clients with dissociative disorders and C-PTSD often experience suicidal ideation; some make gestures or attempts, and there are some who kill themselves. They have many risk factors including severe hopelessness, family messages about death, history of wishing they were dead, parts who are living in the past, and a history of being threatened with death and/or witnessing it. It is important to work on understanding the motivation of the suicidal parts, as there are many including: suicide as a relief from pain and torment, as a punishment for being "evil", as having the ultimate control, and as a delusion of separateness where one part can kill another and live. One client said, *"When we kill the bad, weak asshole who got us abused, we will be safe and feel great."*

In a New England Society for the Treatment of Trauma and Dissociation meeting, Christine Courtois, PhD discussed suicide. Here are 3 of her points:

1. "There are 2 kinds of therapists. The ones who've had one or more clients suicide and the ones who will." Somehow in grad school I got the impression that if I did everything right no one would ever kill themselves. This kind of fallacy can lead to therapists having excessive shame when they actually have done good work. It is important to be accurate about what we have control and responsibility for and what we don't.

2. Courtois suggests early on in treatment communicating a statement crafted from Job's book: *Managing Suicidal Risk* (2006): *"Our contract is to work on you staying alive and healing. If you decide you do not want that anymore, and it's your decision, you need to end treatment"*
3. Risk Management: If there is a suicide or homicide, call your malpractice insurance company and inform them. Courtois suggests the best defense is to have had a thoughtful process that is charted including when you have had consultation on the client's therapy.

The Compass of Shame (Nathanson, 1992)

Shame thrives in secrecy and can be so painful that it often needs to be brought up by the therapist. In addition to normal shame and the shame that normally occurs as a byproduct of abuse and neglect, abusive people often project their own shame onto their victims.

Understanding the four points on the Compass of Shame helps us notice these patterns in our clients, and perhaps ourselves. It is important to notice how these patterns function in the client's relationships with others and to notice these patterns in the relationships among the parts.

The Four Points on the Compass of Shame Are:

- **Attack Self:** The client or part berates themselves with statements like, *"I'm no good, I'm disgusting, I'm a piece of shit."* Or there may be a part who physically attacks themselves or other parts.
- **Attack Others:** Shame can be externalized by blaming and attacking others, including the therapist. Critical/perpetrator-identified parts attack other parts.

One motivation is to "prevent failure" by shutting up vulnerable parts.
- **Avoid Others:** A client or part thinks "I don't need friends." They use avoidance to protect themselves from feeling shame.
- **Avoidance of Inner Experience**: Denial of or distracting from shame can take the shape of joking, storytelling, or having endless crises to avoid the pain of dealing with shame and the traumas that caused it.

Conclusion

There are many complexities in working with clients with complex trauma disorders. This chapter is a potpourri of important information I wish I'd known about sooner in my career. There is no particular organization or conclusions to be had from this chapter, other than, there is always more to learn and that is what keeps things interesting.

CHAPTER 16
Afterword

The first training I participated in on dissociation was with Richard Kluft, MD. I thought what he taught was perfect and I couldn't imagine that any other method would ever be necessary. One of the many insightful things he said to my dismay was, "in 20 years therapists will have figured out different ways of working that will be even more useful." He was presenting the technology of the time, and there would be new and even better technology. Every cell of my body said, "*No This is the answer.*" I wanted that certainty, I wanted to be in the know, and to have the absolute answer. There is a part of me that still likes the idea of a perfect answer, but I have found that a greater perfection lies in curiosity, collaboration, compassion, and more curiosity. How much more interesting life and work is, having a foundation of competence and from there to be open and curious.

Internal Family Systems is a system that has opened doors in my mind, made me more flexible, and added a richness to my work. It is also a system with its own vocabulary and world view. It is very powerful and has had an enormous impact. That power comes with a tendency to close doors to anyone who doesn't follow the path, to heighten the perceived error of outsider ways, and

Afterword

to block any external knowledge. Does one size really fit them all as Procrustes* required, or can there be room for difference, collaboration, and a wider view.

> **Procrustes:** In Greek mythology, Procrustes was a thief who killed his victims by forcing them to lie on a bed, and then making tall victims fit the bed perfectly by chopping parts of their bodies off, or stretching victims who were too short. (Merriam Webster Dictionary)

The population with dissociative disorders has been left out of the expansive yet limited system of IFS. Therapists who are trained in IFS and trained to think that all you need is IFS are at times unknowingly working with dissociative disorder clients. Not all, but many of these clients are suffering. These clinicians for the most part receive consultation from IFS consultants who are experts in IFS, and who give them IFS answers. IFS, which is so powerful and right for so many people, may be the right path, but it does not always go far enough. It leaves clinicians and clients to continue their struggle to find the magic of IFS, from within a box that is constructed and constrained by IFS, sure that the IFS answer is somewhere.

Four of the Cs speak directly towards being truly in Self with regard to growth and development:

- Curiosity to look comprehensively at ways of helping people,
- Courage to go outside the box,
- Connectedness to competence and knowledge of fields outside of IFS, and

- Clarity when a client is struggling and continuing to suffer and needs a different answer.

There is a part of me that wishes this book could be all you need, but in Self, I know it is incomplete, a beginning or a space from which you, the reader, can continue growing. Let the information from this book percolate, think of it in relation to your clients and yourself, then, when necessary, start with references in the appendix and see where you might want to go from there. Every time I learn, my clients benefit energetically and clinically The resonance from my learning transmits a message to them that change and growth are positive and expansive. Additionally, our ability to look at and sit with the unknown helps our clients to take radical steps away from the dysfunctional systems in their families of origin and move forward towards leading a life that is not defined by the traumas and neglect from the past, towards integrated functioning and a Self-led life.

Afterword

People are like this tree whose growth was inhibited by
burdens inflicted during its youth. As soon as it was freed,
it could live as it would have without the burdens. The
existence of childhood remains, but once healed, the trunk
developed in its youth becomes a very strong foundation.

Appendix

This appendix provides additional resources and material on the subject material. Please note that websites listed were available at time of publishing but may be subject to change. This section includes:

- DSM V Categories for Dissociative Disorders
- Sources for Training and Further information
- Recommended Reading
- Self-Help Books for Complex Trauma Survivors
- Screening Self Report Questionnaires and Diagnostic Interviews
- Handout for Safe Space Imagery
- Glossary of Initials
- Glossary

DSM V Diagnostic Categories for Dissociative Disorders

This book is primarily written about treating DID, OSDD, and C-PTSD. This list gives all the DSM V categories for dissociative disorders. It is recommended that you have some familiarity with them so if you see some kind of dissociative symptomology, you will be able to recognize it.

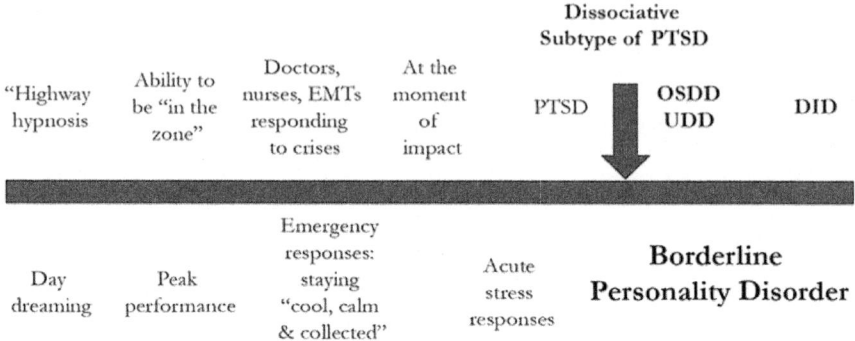

The Dissociative Continuum shows the range of dissociation from normal to diagnostic.

- 300.14: Dissociative Identity Disorder
- 300.12: Dissociative Amnesia including Dissociative Fugue
- 300.6: Depersonalization-Derealization syndrome
    - Depersonalization: Experiences of unreality detachment, or being an outside observer with respect to one's thoughts, feelings, sensations, body or actions.
    - Derealization: Experiences of unreality or detachment with respect to surroundings.
    - One excellent resource is the book: Simeon, D., Abugel, J. (2006). *Feeling Unreal: Depersonalization Disorder and the Loss of the Self.* Oxford, England: Oxford University Press.

Appendix

- 300.16: Other Specified Dissociative Disorder (previously known as Dissociative Disorder Not Otherwise Specified (DDNOS)
- 300.15: Unspecified Dissociative Disorder (UDD)
- 300.11: Dissociative Disorders of movement or sensation
  - Includes: conversion disorders, pseudoseizures, sensory loss
- 309.81: Posttraumatic Stress Disorder, dissociative subtype

> Note: DID is sometimes easily diagnosed, but all dissociative disorders need to be diagnosed and validated over time, as the childhood need to keep things hidden and dissociated can mask symptoms. Conversion disorders, and Depersonalization-derealization syndrome are at times, for instance, the outward manifestation of DID. Other times, they are just what they are.

- The diagnosis Complex Post Traumatic Stress Disorder is listed in the International Classification of Diseases. 11th Edition.

Sources for Training and Further Information

- American Society of Clinical Hypnosis: www.asch.net.
- Internal Family Systems Institute: https://ifs-institute.com.
- International Society for the Treatment of Trauma and Dissociation: www.ISST-D.org
  - Treating Dissociative Disorders 101: www.isst-d.org/education/dissociation-101.htm

Recommended Reading for Further Learning

This section is not comprehensive, but these are great references to start out with or add to what you have already read. They are highly recommended.

Brand, BL., Schielke, HJ., Schiavone, F., Lanius, RA. (2022). *Overcoming Obstacles in Trauma Treatment.* Cary, NC: Oxford University Press.

Chu, J. A., et al. (2011). "Guidelines for treating dissociative identity disorder in adults, third revision." *Journal of Trauma & Dissociation*, 12(2): 115–187. Web URL: www.isst-d.org/jtd/2011AdultTreatmentGuidelinesSummary.pdf

Boon, S., Steele, K., van der Hart, O. (2011). *Coping with Trauma-Related Dissociation: Skills Training for Patients and Therapists.* New York, NY: Norton and Company.

Salter, A.C. (1995). *Transforming Trauma: A Guide to Understanding and Treating Adult Survivors of Child Sexual Abuse.* Newbury Park, CA: Sage Press.

Steele, K., Boon, S., and van der Hart, O., (2017). *Treating Trauma-Related Dissociation.* New York, NY: W.W. Norton and Company, Inc.

Schwartz, H.L., (1993). *The Alchemy of Wolves and Sheep: A Relational Approach to Internalized Perpetration in Complex Trauma Survivors.* London and NY: Routledge.

Five Self Help Books Written for Complex Trauma

These books are great to have on your shelf to use with clients. I advise that clients read and work with them and/or if a client cannot read them on their own, I read sections to them and we work on reading passages together.

Boon, S., Steele, K., van der Hart, O. (2011). *Coping with Trauma-Related Dissociation: Skills Training for Patients and Therapists.* New York, NY: Norton and Company.

Brown, LS. (2012). *Your Turn for Care: Surviving the aging and death of the adults who harmed you.*

Brown, LS. (2015). *Not the price of Admission: Healthy relationships after childhood trauma.*

Courtois, C.A. (2014, 2020). *It's Not You, It's What Happened To You.* Dublin, Ohio: Telemachus Press, LLC.

Emerald, D. 2009. *The Power of Ted* (*The Empowerment Dynamic).* Virginia: Polaris Publishing. Note: This book is about the Karpman Drama Triangle (Persecutor, Rescuer, Victim) and its resolution. It's written as a fable and may seem odd to some, but the heart of the book is very clear and useful. It has helped people identify which role they are in and how to stay out of them. Some of my complex DID clients have used it to make progress in their marriage.

Screening Self-Report Questionnaires Available Online:

Carlson, E.B. & Putnam, F.W. (1993). An update on the Dissociative Experience Scale. *Dissociation.* 6(1), p. 16-27. Web URL: Dissociative Experiences Scale (DES-II): Screening for Dissociative Identity Disorder and more (traumadissociation.com)

Waller et al., (1996) Dissociative Experience Scale-Taxon (DES-T). Web URL: http://www.isst-d.org/default.asp?contentID=66 (The DES-Taxon relates to the 8 most significant questions on the DES.)

Dell, P. (2006). "The Multidimensional Inventory of Dissociation" *Journal of Trauma & Dissociation.* 7(2):77-106. Web URL:

Web Home of the MID | Developed by Paul F. Dell, PhD (mid-assessment.com).

Nijenhuis, E. (2011). "Somatoform Dissociation Questionnaire (SDQ) 20 and 5. Web URL: www.enijenhuis.nl

Diagnostic Interviews Available Online:

Ross, C. (1989). "The Dissociative Disorders Interview Schedule." *Dissociation.* Vol II. No3. 169-189. Web URL: www.rossinst.com

Steinberg, M. (1995). *Structured Clinical Interview for DSM-IV Dissociative Disorders (SCID-D).* 2nd *Revised Edition.* Washington, DC: American Psychiatric Association Publishing. Web URL: (PDF) Advances in the clinical assessment of dissociation: The SCID-D-R (researchgate.net)

Abbreviations

CBT: Cognitive Behavioral Treatment

C-PTSD: Complex PTSD

DES: Dissociative Experience Scale

DSM: Diagnostic and Statistical Manual of Mental Disorders

DD: Disorder Disordered

DID: Dissociative Identity Disorder

DDIS: Dissociative Disorder Interview Schedule

DDNOS: Dissociative Disorder Not Other Specified, Is the DSM's previous diagnosis for DSM 5's OSDD.

E.G.: Latin abbreviation for "Such as"

EMDR: Eye Movement Desensitization and Reprocessing

EMDR Trauma and Recovery HAP: EMDR Trauma and Recovery Humanitarian Assistance Program

ICD: The International Classification of Diseases

I.E.: Latin abbreviation for "That is"

IFS: Internal Family Systems

ISSTD: The International Society for the Treatment of Trauma and Dissociation

MPD: Multiple Personality Disorder, now known as DID

PIP: Picture in a Picture TV Technology

PRN: Pro Re Nata translated from Latin means "use as needed." It is used in reference to medication.

PTSD: Post Traumatic Stress Disorder

OSDD: Other Specified Personality Disorder, formerly known as DDNOS (Dissociative Disorder Not Other Specified in DSM-4)

SCID-D: Structured Clinical Interview for DSM-IV Dissociative Disorders

SSI: Safe Space Imagery

SUD: Subjective Units of Distress

UDD: Unspecified Dissociative Disorder

Glossary

- **Backlash:** Backlash is defined as a "strong and adverse reaction." IFS uses this word to describe when something isn't attended to sufficiently in session and a firefighter comes out and disrupts functioning. This may occur when concerns are not fully addressed, a manager gets overwhelmed, an exile is triggered, etc. In terms of treating clients with complex trauma disorders, backlash can also be used to describe what happens when a client's coping skills get overwhelmed.
- **Blending**: Blending occurs when a part (or parts) blends with Self resulting in Self energy being partially to completely unavailable. You can tell you or a client is blended when qualities of Self are not present. See the **8 Cs** below.
- **Burdens**: Traumatic material, beliefs, etc. that are carried by parts including exiles, managers, and firefighters
- **8 Cs**: Refers to the 8 qualities of Self: compassion, curiosity, clarity, creativity, calm, confidence, courage and connectedness

- **Cis Gender**: a cis gendered person is a person whose sense of gender and identity corresponds with their birth sex.
- **Cognitive Behavioral Therapy (CBT)**: CBT is a kind of talk therapy that helps people restructure and change negative and habitual thinking patterns and behaviors.
- **Complex Post Traumatic Stress Disorder (C-PTSD)**: C-PTSD is a developmental trauma disorder which forms in response to repeated interpersonal violence and neglect that results in the child feeling hopeless, helpless, and often a fear of death. It is a descriptive term, not a DSM 5 diagnosis.
- **Critical Mass of Self energy**: Being 100% in Self is not required. Having enough Self energy, or a critical mass of Self energy is. Often when working with clients with C-PTSD and DDs it is important to work to identify small amounts of Self energy and build on that. Examples of small important amounts of Self energy include a client recognizing the presence of a part, and a client acknowledging that they are not ready to work with a part but are aware it is there and will work with it when the time is right. Thus, Acknowledging/noticing the presence of a part is an attribute of Self.
- **Depersonalization**: Not feeling attached to oneself or a part of oneself, or a sense of not being real.
- **Derealization**: Not feeling attached to one's environment.
- **Diagnostic and Statistical Manual**: The DSM is the handbook for mental health diagnosis used in the USA.
- **Direct Access**: Direct Access is the IFS term for working with parts directly. It is how therapists successfully work with clients with complex trauma disorders when they do not do IFS.

- **Dissociation**: Dissociation refers to what happens when something usually connected or associated is disconnected or dissociated. E.g., knowledge, feelings, and sensations of a traumatic event can be dissociated. The DSM-5 lists dissociation occurring in the realms of consciousness, memory, identity, or perception.
- **Dissociative Identity Disorder (DID) and Other Specified Dissociative Disorder (OSDD)** are the two dissociative disorders primarily discussed in this book.
- **Dissociative Disorders**: Dissociative Disorders are a classification of disorders developed by children who have been variously abused, neglected, abandoned, and/or had parents with severe attachment disorders.
- **Exiles:** Is the IFS term for parts who have been dissociated or pushed away from consciousness to protect the system from their burdens of traumatic material. They are often child parts.
- **Ego State**s: "Are normal phenomena that we all experience, and they do not indicate the presence of a dissociative disorder. They differ from dissociative parts in their lack of autonomy and elaboration, personal experience and memory, and unique self-representation and first-person perspective." (Steele, et al. 2017) An IFS way of describing them might be Healthy Normal Multiplicity. This definition differentiates parts from ego states, although, at times, people refer to parts casually as ego states and do not differentiate them.
- **Eye Movement Desensitization and Reprocessing (EMDR):** is a powerful therapy model, developed by Francine Shapiro, PhD. One hallmark of EMDR is that it uses bilateral eye movement, tapping, and/or tones.

- **Firefighters:** Are parts who reflexively react when exiles are triggered, and managers overwhelmed. They react quickly to calm or numb out the exile, or to distract from it. They tend to use extreme ways to do this, e.g., self-destructive behaviors, drinking, drugs, excessive eating, and dissociating.
- **Fragments:** Fragments (parts who consist of a bit of history, feeling, sensation, etc.), and parts who do not have a range of feelings and experiences. All parts are critical for healing as are fragments.
- **ICD-10:** The 10th revision of the international Statistical Classification of Diseases and Related Health Problems. (World Health Organization) It is used widely throughout the world. The USA uses their own version, the DSM, when diagnosing mental disorders.
- **Internal Family Systems (IFS):** (See Chapter 2)
- **Managers:** An IFS term for parts who manage daily life and protect the system from burdens and parts who carry them.
- **Multiple Personality Disorder (MPD):** The previous diagnosis for DID
- **Normal Multiplicity**: Normal Multiplicity is an IFS term for the awareness that all people have parts. This awareness is consistent with other ego state models, although IFS also includes the concept of Self.
- **Orienting to the Present:** Parts often feel like they live in the past. They may be partially aware of things about the present and still be anchored in the past. Orienting to the present means helping them move from the past into the present. It is similar to IFS's concept of Retrieval. (See Chapter 11, Section 3.)

- **Parts:** IFS defines parts as inner people/subpersonalities. In the Trauma and Dissociation field, parts have a wider definition and include fragments (parts who consist of a bit of history, feeling, sensation, etc.), and parts who do not have a range of feelings and experiences.
- **Polarization**: Polarization occurs when 2 parts (or 2 groups of parts) believe the opposite of each other.
- **Projective Identification**: Is a defense mechanism where a person projects an unwanted feeling or characteristic on the other person. It can also be a mode of nonverbal communication.
- **Internal System**: Refers to the internal system of parts within a person.
- **Reenactments**: Reenactments are patterns of past behavior/circumstance/trauma that get unconsciously cocreated between the client and the therapist. They consist of unconscious material from both client and therapist. It is also a mode of nonverbal communication.
- **Retrieval**: In IFS retrieval is taking an exile out of the past after it has been witnessed. In Trauma Informed IFS retrieval or orienting to the present is done when necessary with all parts who have been existing partially or totally in the past. This could be before or after Witnessing. (See Chapter 11, Section 3)
- **Self**: The IFS concept of the core of a person. You can tell if you or a client is in Self if they have leadership qualities (curiosity, compassion, confidence, etc.) in relation to parts and/or others. Everyone has a Self. Self is not a part and it is always there however obscured by parts.
- **Self energy**: Self energy can be 100% or less. A part can also have Self energy.

- **Self-led**: A person is Self-led when they live and respond from Self. Parts have input but respect Self's leadership.
- **Subjective Units of Distress** (SUD): A scale from 0 to 10 where zero equates to no distress and 10 equates to the maximum amount of distress possible
- **Traumatic material:** Another term for burdens carried by parts.
- **Unblending**: When parts are blended with Self, the goal is to have them unblend so Self or an amount of Self energy is present.
- **Unburdening**: Parts letting go of traumatic material.
- **Window of Tolerance**: Concept developed in 1999 by Dan Siegel, MD to describe the optimal range of arousal to function in daily life. How to Help Your Clients Understand Their Window of Tolerance (nicabm.com)
- **Witnessing: Is an** IFS term for when an unblended part communicates what it wants Self to know about it. This includes traumatic material, experiences, feelings, etc. Once the part is fully witnessed, it can often be unburdened.

Bibliography

Abugel, J., and Simeon, D. 2006. *Feeling Unreal: Depersonalization Disorder and the Loss of the Self.* Oxford, England: Oxford University Press.

Anderson, F.G., Schwartz, R.C., and Sweezy, M. 2017. *Internal Family Systems: Skills Training Manual. Trauma-Informed Treatment for Anxiety, Depression, PTSD & Substance Ab*use. Eau Claire, Wisconsin: PESI Publishing and Media.

Anderson, F.G. 2021. *Transcending Trauma: Healing Complex PTSD with Internal Family Systems Therapy.* Eau Claire, Wisconsin: PESI Publishing and Media.

Armstrong, Brand, B., and Loewenstein, R. 2006. "Psychological Assessment of Patients with Dissociative Identity Disorder." *The Psychiatric Clinics of North America.* 29. 145-68. Web URL: (PDF) Psychological Assessment of Patients with Dissociative Identity Disorder (researchgate.net)

Barach, P. M., Boon, S., Bowman, E. S., Brand, B., Cardeña, E., Chefetz, R.A., Chu, J. A., Classen, C., Coons, P. M., Courtois,

C. A., Dalenberg, C. J., Dell, P. F., Dorahy, M., Fine,C.G., Frankel, A. S., Gast, U., Gelinas,D.J., Gold, S. N., Golston, J. C., Goodwin, G., Howell, E., Jacobson-Levy, M., Kluft, R. P., Loewenstein, R.J., Middleton, W., Nijenhuis, E. R. S., Paulsen, S., Ross, C. A., Sar,V., Somer, E., Steele, K., Twombly, J., Van der Hart, O., and Young, L. M. 2011. "Guidelines for treating dissociative identity disorder in adults, third revision." *Journal of Trauma & Dissociation*, 12(2): 115–187.

Baker, S. 1998. "Dancing the Dance with Dissociatives: Some thoughts on countertransference, projective identification and enactments in the treatment of dissociative disorders." *Dissociation.* Volume 10, No. 4, p. 214-222

Berne, E. 1961. *Transactional Analysis in Psychotherapy*. New York, NY: Grove Press.

Boon, S., Steele, K., van der Hart, O. 2011. *Coping with Trauma-Related Dissociation: Skills Training for Patients and Therapists.* New York, NY: Norton and Company.

Boon, S., Steele, K., and Van der Hart, O. 2017. *Treating Trauma-Related Dissociation.* New York, NY: W.W. Norton and Company, Inc.

Brand, B.L., Chasson, G.S., Lanius, R.A., Leventhal, B., and Myrick, A.C. 2015. "Treatment of Complex Dissociative Disorders: A Comparison of Interventions Reported by Community Therapists versus Those Recommended by Experts." *Journal of Trauma & Dissociation*, 16:1, 51-67

Brand, B.L., Loewenstein, R.J., and Spiegel, D. 2014. "Dispelling Myths About Dissociative Identity Disorder Treatment: An Empirically Based Approach." *Psychiatry.* 77(2).

Brand, B.L., **and** Lowenstein, R.J. 2014. "Does Phasic Trauma Treatment Make Patients With Dissociative Identity Disorder Treatment More Dissociative?" *Journal of Trauma & Dissociation.* 15(1):52-65

Braun, B.G. 1988. "The BASK model of dissociation." *Dissociation.* 1, 4-24. Web URL:

https://scholarsbank.uoregon.edu/xmlui/handle/1794/1340

Brown, D.P., and Fromm, E. 1986. *Hypnotherapy and Hypnoanalysis.* New Jersey: Lawrence Erlbaum Associates, Inc.

Brown, L.S. 2015. *Not the Price of Admission: Healthy Relationships after Childhood Trauma .*

Burns, D.W. 1980. *Feeling Good: The New Mood Therapy.* New York, NY: William Morrow and Company.

Carlson, EB., and Putnam, FW. 1993. "Dissociative Experiences *Scale-II* (DES-II)" Web URL: Microsoft Word - Dissociative Experiences Scale II with description and Interpretation.doc (weebly.com)

Chu, J.C. 1998. *Rebuilding Shattered Lives: The Responsible Treatment of Complex Post-Traumatic and Dissociative Disorders.* New York, NY: John Wiley and Sons, Inc.

Cloitre, M. 2020. ICD-11 complex post-traumatic stress disorder: simplifying diagnosis in trauma populations. *The British Journal of Psychiatry.* 216, 129–131.

Courtois, C. A. 1999. *Recollections of Sexual Abuse: Treatment Principles and Guidelines.* New York, NY: W.W. Norton.

Dalenberg, C. 2000. *Countertransference and the Treatment of Trauma.* Washington, D.C.: American Psychological Association.

Davies, J.M., and Frawley, M.G. 1994. "Eight transference countertransference positions." In: *Treating the Adult Survivor of Childhood Sexual Abuse.* New York, NY: Basic Books.

De Becker, G. 1998. *The Gift of Fear and Other Survival Signals That Protect Us From Violence.* New York, NY: Dell Publishing.

Dell, P.F. 2006. "The Multidimensional Inventory of Dissociation (MID): A Comprehensive measure of pathological dissociation." *Journal of Trauma & Dissociation.* 7(2): 77-106. Web URL: Web Home of the MID | Developed by Paul F. Dell, PhD (mid-assessment.com).

Dell, P. F., Lewis-Fernandez, R., Loewenstein, R. J., Sar, V., Simeon, D., Spiegel, D., and Vermetten, E. 2011. "Dissociative disorders in DSM-5." *Official Journal of the Anxiety and Depression Association of America.* 28, 824–852.

American Psychiatric Association. 2013. *Diagnostic and statistical manual of mental disorders* (5th ed.). Washington, DC: American Psychiatric Association.

Brand, B.L., Dorahy, M.J., Krüger, C., Martínez-Taboas, A., Middleton, W., Şar, V., and Sand tavropoulos, P. 2014. *Dissociative Identity Disorder: An empirical overview.* Web URL: Dorahy_Dissociative_2014.pdf (up.ac.za)

Ducey, C.P., and Van der Kolk, B.A. 1989. "The Psychological Processing of Traumatic Experience: Rorschach Patterns in PTSD". *Journal of Traumatic Stress.* Vol. 2(3), 259-273. Wiley.

Emerald, D. 2009. *The Power of Ted* (*The Empowerment Dynamic)*. Virginia: Polaris Publishing.

Fine, C.G. (1991). "Treatment stabilization and crisis prevention: Pacing the therapy of the multiple personality disorder patient." *Psychiatric Clinics of North America*, 14, 661- 676.

Erickson, M. 1980. "The nature of hypnosis and suggestion: The collected papers of Milton H. Erickson on hypnosis." (Vol.1, E.L. Rossi, Ed.) New York, NY: Irvington.

Federn, P. 1952. *Ego Psychology and the Psychoses*. New York, NY: Basic Books.

Frankel, A.S. PhD., JD. 2009. "Dissociation and dissociative disorders: clinical and forensic assessment." In Dell, P. F., & O'Neil, J. A. (Eds.). *Dissociation and the Dissociative Disorders: DSM-V and Beyond*. New York, NY: Routledge.

Fraser, G.A. 2003. "Fraser's dissociative table technique' revisited, revised: a strategy for working with ego states in dissociative disorder and ego state therapy." *Journal of Trauma and Dissociation*. 4:4.5-28.

Frederick, C. and McNeal, S. 1999. *Inner Strengths: Contemporary Psychotherapy and Hypnosis for Ego-Strengthening*. New Jersey: Lawrence Erlbaum Associates, Publishers.

Frewen, P.A., and Lanius, R. A., 2014. "Trauma Related Altered States of Consciousness: Exploring the 4-D Model." *Journal of Trauma and Dissociation*. 15:436-456. New York, NY: Routledge: Taylor and Francis Group.

Gray, J. 2001. *What You Feel You Can Heal*. Farringdon, London: Pan Macmillan.

Hassan, S. 2016. *Combating Cult Mind Control.* Newton, MA: Freedom of Mind Press.

Hassan, S. 2000. *The BITE Model of Destructive Mind Control,* Web URL: BITE Model Analysis—Examining Unsafe Groups and Leaders (wordpress.com)

Herman, J.L. 1992 and 1997. *Trauma and Recovery: The Aftermath of Violence--From Domestic Abuse to Political Terror.* New York: NY. Basic Books.

Holmes, T. 2011. *Parts Work: An Illustrated Guide to Your Inner Life,* Kalamazoo, MI: Winged Heart Press.

Howell, E. 2011. *Understanding and Treating Dissociative Identity Disorder: A Relational Approach.* New York, NY: Routledge.

International Classification of Diseases 11 (ICD-11). 2018. World Health Organization .

Janet, P. 1925, reprinted in 2019. *A Historical and Clinical Study-Volume One and Two.* Eastford, CT: Martino FINE Books.

Jobs, D. 2006. *Managing Suicidal Risk.* New York, NY: The Guilford Press.

Kahler, JA. And Turkus, J.A. 2006. "Therapeutic interventions in the treatment of dissociative disorders." *Psychiatric Clinics of North Am.* 2006 Mar;29(1):245-62.

Karpman, S. 1968. "Fairy tales and script drama analysis." Transactional Analysis Bulletin, 7(26), 39-43. Web URL: The Official Site of the Karpman Drama Triangle

Kluft, R,P. 1987. "The Parental Fitness of Mothers with Multiple Personality Disorder: a Preliminary Study." *Child Abuse and Neglect.* 11(2):273-80.

Kluft, R.P. 1992. "Hypnosis with Multiple Personality Disorder." *American Journal of Preventive Psychiatry and Neurology.* 3, 19-27.

Kluft, R.P. 1989. "Playing for Time: Temporizing Techniques in the Treatment of Multiple Personality Disorder." *American Journal of Clinical Hypnosis*, 32:2, 90-98

Kluft, R.P., and Fine, C.G. 1993. *Clinical Perspectives on Multiple Personality Disorder.* Washington, DC and London, England: American Psychiatric Press, Inc.

Kluft, R.P. 1999. "Current Issues in Dissociative Identity Disorder." *Journal of Practical Psychiatry and Behavioral Health, 3-19.* (The name of this journal is now the *Journal of Psychiatric Practice.)*

Kluft, R.P. 1994. "Applications of hypnotic interventions." *Hypnos.* 21, 205-223.

Lanius, R., Miller, M., Wolf, E., Brand, B., Frewen, P., Vermetten, E., and Spiegel, D. 2019. *Dissociative Subtype of PTSD.* PTSD. Dissociative Subtype of PTSD - PTSD: National Center for PTSD (va.gov)

Liotti, G. 1999. "Disorganized attachment as a model for understanding dissociative psychopathology." In J. Solomon & C. George (Eds.), *Attachment disorganization* (pp. 297-243). New York, NY: Guilford.

Lown, B. 1999. *The Lost Art of Healing: Practicing Compassion in Medicine.* N.Y., New York, NY: Random House USA Inc.

Ludwig, A.M. 1966. "Altered states of consciousness." *Archives of General Psychiatry*, 15, 225-234.

Luxenberg, T., Spinazzola, J., and van der Kolk, B. 2001. "Complex Trauma and Disorders of Extreme Stress (DESNOS) Diagnosis, Part Two: Treatment." *Directions in Psychiatry.* Volume 21. (PDF) Complex Trauma and Disorders of Extreme Stress (DESNOS) Diagnosis, Part Two: Treatment (researchgate.net).

Lyons-Ruth, K. and Jacobvitz, D. 1999. "Attachment disorganization: Unresolved loss, relational violence, and lapses in behavioral and attentional strategies." In: J. Cassidy and P.R. Shaver (Hg.): *Handbook of Attachment: Theory, research, and clinical applications* (pp 520-554) New York, NY: Guilford.

Lyons-Ruth K. 2003. "The Two-Person Construction of Defenses: Disorganized Attachment Strategies, Unintegrated Mental States, and Hostile/Helpless Relational Processes." *Journal of Infant, Child, and Adolescent Psychotherapy.* 2:105-114.

Maercker, A. 2021. Development of the new CPTSD diagnosis for ICD-11. *Borderline personality disorder and emotion dysregulation*, 8(1), 7.

Main, M., Kaplan, N., and Cassidy, J. 1985. *Security in infancy, childhood, and adulthood: A move to the level of representation.* Monographs of the Society for Research in Child Development, 50, 66-104.

Maslow, A. (1962). *Toward a Psychology of Being.* New York: NY: Van Nostrand Reinhold.

Morton, P., and Frederick, C. 1997. "Intrapsychic transitional space: A resource for integration in hypnotherapy." *Hypnos*, 24, 32-41.

Nathanson, D.L. 1992. *Shame and Pride: Affect, Sex, and the Birth of Self.* New York, NY: Norton.

Nijenhuis, E. 2011. "Somatoform Dissociation Questionnaire (SDQ) 20 and 5. In Chu, JA. *Rebuilding Shattered Lives, Second Edition.* Hoboken, NJ: John Wiley & Sons, Inc. Web URL: www.enijenhuis.nl

Nijenhuis, E. 2004. "Trauma-related structural dissociation of the personality." Trauma Information Pages website, January 2004. Web URL: http://www.trauma-pages.com/nijenhuis-2004.htm

Nijenhuis, E., Steele, K., and Van der Hart, O. 2006. *The Haunted Self: Structural Dissociation and the Treatment of Chronic Traumatization.* New York, NY: Norton.

Nijenhuis, E., Steele, K., and Van der Hart, O. 2001. "Posttraumatic Stress Disorders and Dissociative Disorders" Originally, published in: *Journal of Trauma and Dissociation*,

2(4), 79-116. Web URL: http://www.trauma-pages.com/articles.htm

Pelcovitz, D., Roth, S., Spinazzola, J., Sunday, S., and Van der Kolk, B.A. 2005. *Disorders of Extreme Stress: The Empirical Foundation of a Complex Adaptation to Trauma.* Journal of Traumatic Stress, Vol. 18, No. 5, 389–399.

Rodberg, G. 2005. *"Treating Mother's With Dissociative Identity Disorder."* International Society for the Study of Trauma and Dissociation, Annual Conference Presentation.

Ross, C. 1989. "The Dissociative Disorders Interview Schedule." *Dissociation.* Vol II. No3. 169-189. Web URL: www.rossinst.com

Saad, L. 2020. *Me and White Supremacy: Combat Racism, Change the World, and Become a Good Ancestor.* Naperville, Illinois: Sourcebooks.

Salter, A.C. 1995. *Transforming Trauma: A Guide to Understanding and Treating Adult Survivors of Child Sexual Abuse.* Newbury Park, CA: Sage Press.

Schreiber, F.R. 1973. *Sybil. The Classic True Story of a Woman Possessed by Sixteen Separate Personalities.* Washington, DC: Regnery Publishing.

Schwartz, H.L. 1993. *The Alchemy of Wolves and Sheep: A Relational Approach to Internalized Perpetration in Complex Trauma Survivors.* London and NY: Routledge.

Schwartz, R.C. 1995. *Internal Family Systems Therapy.* New York, NY: Guilford Press.

Schwartz, R.C., and Sweezy, M., 2020. *Internal Family Systems Therapy, Second Edition.* New York, NY. Guilford Press.

Schwartz, R., and Twombly, J.H. 2008. "The Integration of the Internal Family Systems Model and EMDR." In *Healing the Heart of Trauma and Dissociation with EMDR and Ego State Therapy.* Ed. Forgash, C. and Copley, M. New York, NY: Springer Publishing.

Schnall, M., and Steinberg, M. 2001. *The Stranger in the Mirror*. New York, NY: Harper Collins.

Steinberg, M. 1995. *Structured Clinical Interview for DSM-IV Dissociative Disorders (SCID-D). 2nd Revised Edition.* Washington, DC: American Psychiatric Association Publishing.

Stone, H., and Stone, S. 1989. *Embracing Each Other: Relationship As Teacher, Healer & Guide.* Oakland, CA: New World Library.

Twombly, J.H. 2001. "Safe Place Imagery: Handling Intrusive Thoughts and Feelings." *The EMDRIA Newsletter: Special Edition*, December, EMDRIA.

Twombly, J.H. 2005. " EMDR for Client's with Dissociative Identity Disorder, DDNOS, and Ego States."

In R. Shapiro (Ed.), *EMDR Solutions: Pathways to Healing.* New York, NY: Norton.

Twombly, J.H. 2010. "Installation and Transmission of Current Time and Life Orientation;" "Height Orientation;" "Safe Space Imagery;" "Installing Therapist, Therapist's Office, and Maintaining Duality;" "Initial Targeting of Traumatic Material." Chapters in *EMDR Scripted Protocols: Special Populations.* Ed. Luber, M. New York, NY: Springer Publishing Company

Twombly, J.H. 2012. "Overt and Covert Perpetrator Ego States in Dissociative Disordered Patients." In Vogt, R. (Ed.), *Perpetrator Introjects: Psychotherapeutic Diagnostics and Treatment Models.* Kroenging, Germany: Asanger Verlag.

Twombly, J.H. 2013. "Integrating IFS with Phase-oriented Treatment of Dissociative Disordered Clients." In *Internal Family Systems Therapy: Versatility in Application*. Ed. Sweezy, M. and Ziskind, EL. New York, NY: Taylor & Francis/Routledge.

Twombly, J.H. 2013. "The DES and Beyond: Screening for Dissociative Disordered Clients." *Trauma and Recovery: HAP Newsletter*.

Van der Kolk, B.A. 1994 and 2014. *The Body Keeps the Score: Memory and the evolving psychobiology of post traumatic stress*. New York, NY: Viking Penguin.

Watkins, J. and Watkins, H. 1997. *Ego States: Theory and Therapy*. New York, NY: W.W. Norton & Company.

Watkins, H. 1993. "Ego-State Therapy: An Overview." *American Journal of Clinical Hypnosis*. 35(4), 232-240. Taylor and Francis.

Waller et al. 1996. Dissociative Experience Scale-Taxon (DES-T). Web URL: http://www.isst-d.org/default.asp?contentID=66

About the Author

Joanne H. Twombly, MSW, LICSW (Pronouns: she/her/hers) is a psychotherapist in private practice in Arlington, MA. She has over thirty years of experience working with C-PTSD and dissociative disorders, provides trainings and consultation. She has written on EMDR and Dissociative Disorders, EMDR and Internal Family Systems, and on working with perpetrator introjects. Her commitment to helping her clients heal and to providing quality training has resulted in her becoming an EMDR Consultant and a Trauma and Recovery Humanitarian Assistance Program Facilitator, Internal Family Systems Certified, and an American Society for Clinical Hypnosis Consultant. She is a past president of the New England Society for the Study of Trauma and Dissociation. In recognition of her achievements and her service on committees and the Board of the International Society for the Study of Trauma and Dissociation (ISSTD) she was honored with ISSTD's Distinguished Achievement Award and is an ISSTD Fellow.

Printed in Great Britain
by Amazon